Enjoy Coffee2

Coffee Branding & Café Design

0123456789abcdefghijklmnopqrstuvwxyz

NemoFactory

(10359) 1F, 52-11, Ilsan-ro 441 beon-gil, Ilsandong-gu, Goyang-si, Gyeonggi-do, Korea
T_ 82-31-915-1511 / **F_** 82-31-915-1520 / **E_** nemofac@naver.com / **www.**nemofactory.net
ⓒ NemoFactory / **ISBN** 979-11-88529-21-6 (13590) / **Reference** Wikimedia / **Designed by** Joon-hee, Lee

Image_ **Spout**_ Marka Works

Coffee is a brewed drink prepared from roasted coffee beans, which are the seeds of berries from the Coffea plant. The genus Coffea is native to tropical Africa (specifically having its origin in Ethiopia and Sudan) and Madagascar, the Comoros, Mauritius, and Réunion in the Indian Ocean. The plant was exported from Africa to countries around the world. Coffee plants are now cultivated in over 70 countries, primarily in the equatorial regions of the Americas, Southeast Asia, India, and Africa. The two most commonly grown are arabica and robusta. Once ripe, coffee berries are picked, processed, and dried. Dried coffee seeds (referred to as beans) are roasted to varying degrees, depending on the desired flavor. Roasted beans are ground and brewed with near-boiling water to produce coffee as a beverage. Coffee is slightly acidic and has a stimulating effect on humans because of its caffeine content. Coffee is one of the most popular drinks in the world. It can be prepared and presented in a variety of ways (e.g., espresso, French press, café latte, etc.). It is usually served hot, although iced coffee is a popular alternative. Clinical studies indicate that moderate coffee consumption is benign or mildly beneficial in healthy adults, with continuing research on whether long-term consumption lowers the risk of some diseases, although there is generally poor quality of such studies. The earliest credible evidence of coffee-drinking appears in Yemen in southern Arabia in the middle of the 15th century in Sufi shrines. It was here in Arabia that coffee seeds were first roasted and brewed in a similar way to how it is now prepared. Coffee seeds were first exported from East Africa to Yemen, as the Coffea arabica plant is thought to have been indigenous to the former. Yemeni traders took coffee back to their homeland and began to cultivate the seed. By the 16th century, it had reached Persia, Turkey, and North Africa. From there, it spread to Europe and the rest of the world. Brazil is the leading grower of coffee, producing one-third of the world total

Image_ **PROJECT Sangrai 1.0**_ Studio Woork

in 2016. Coffee is a major export commodity: it is the top agricultural export for numerous countries and is among the world's largest legal agricultural exports. It is one of the most valuable commodities exported by developing countries. Green (unroasted) coffee is one of the most traded agricultural commodities in the world. Some controversy is associated with coffee cultivation and the way developed countries trade with developing nations and the impact of its cultivation on the environment, in regards to the clearing of land for coffee-growing and water use. Consequently, the markets for fair trade coffee and organic coffee are expanding.

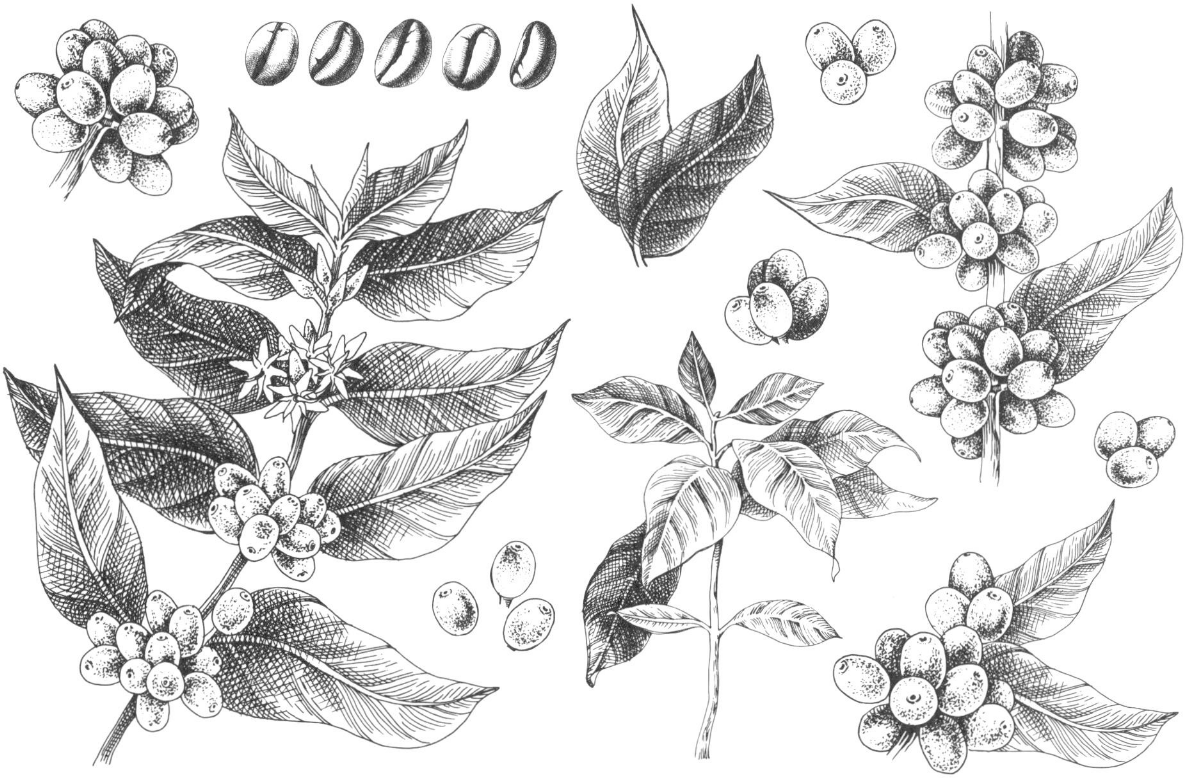

Image_ **Music & Beans**_ Marka Works

The word "coffee" entered the English language in 1582 via the Dutch koffie, borrowed from the Ottoman Turkish kahve, in turn, borrowed from the Arabic qahwah. The Arabic word qahwah was traditionally held to refer to a type of wine whose etymology is given by Arab lexicographers as deriving from the verb qahiya, "to lack hunger", in reference to the drink's reputation as an appetite suppressant. It has also been proposed that the source may be the Proto-Central Semitic root q-h-h meaning "dark". Alternatively, the word Khat, a plant widely used as a stimulant in Yemen and Ethiopia before being supplanted by coffee has been suggested as a possible origin, or the Arabic word quwwah' (meaning "strength"). It may also come from the Kingdom of Kaffa in southeast Ethiopia where Coffea arabica grows wild, but this is considered less likely; in the local Kaffa language, the coffee plant is instead called "bunno". The expression "coffee break" was first attested in 1952. The term "coffee pot" dates from 1705.

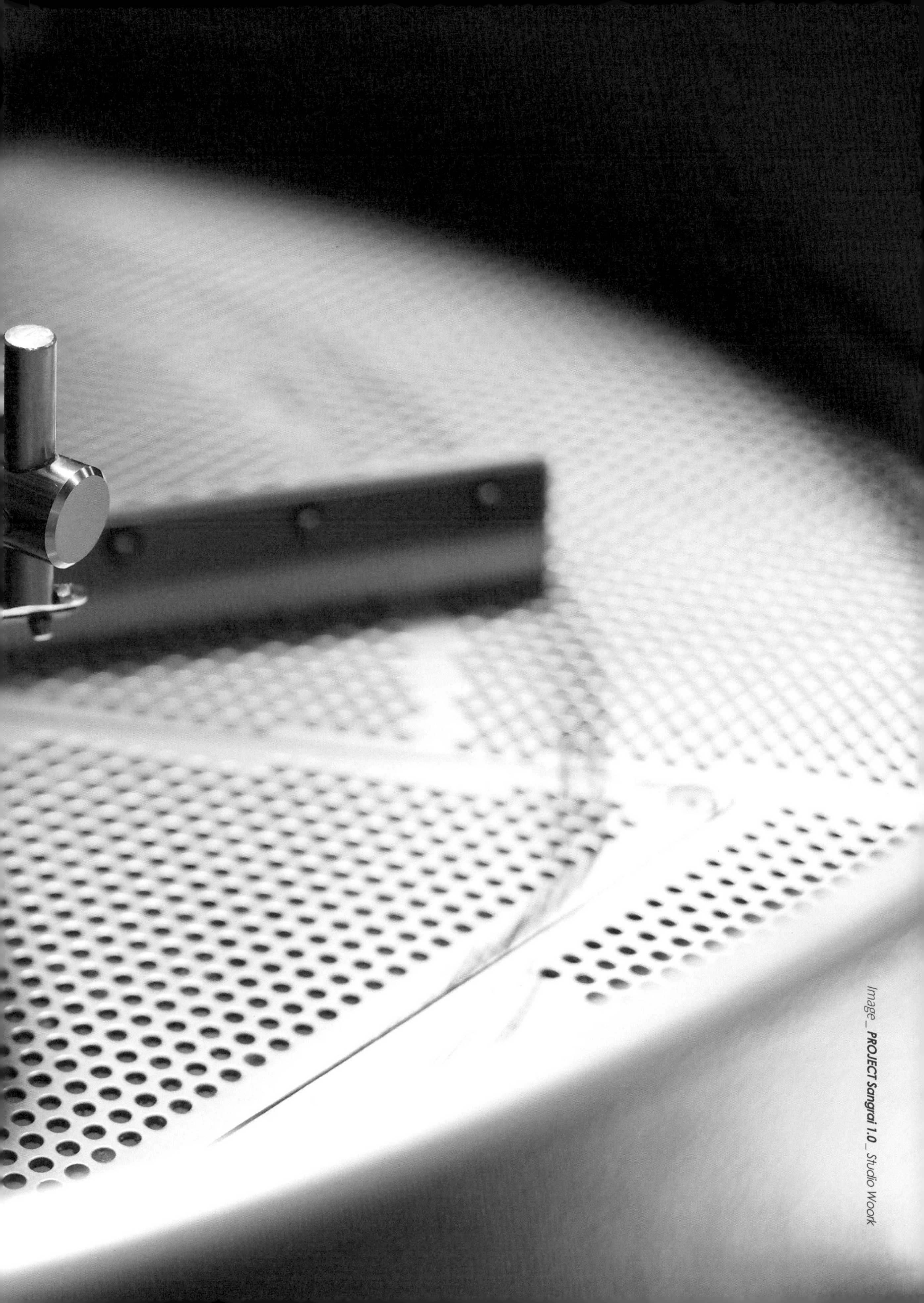

Image_ **PROJECT Sangrai 1.0** _ Studio Woork

Image _ **SINKI HAERO** _ design by 83

Image _ ***Duet Cafe _ Salon*** _ Absence from island

Coffee 커피는 늦어도 9세기부터 에티오피아의 고지대에서 재배되기 시작한 것으로 보인다. 전설에 따르면 염소 목동이었던 칼디(Kaldi)가 우연히 염소들이 먹던 열매를 발견했고 열매를 마을에 가져오면서 피곤함을 덜어주는 커피의 효능을 마을의 종교 수행자들을 돕기 위해 쓰이게 됐다고 전한다. 그곳에서부터 커피는 이집트와 예멘으로 전파되었다. 이집트와 예멘에서는 커피가 종교적 의식에 사용되기도 했다. 15세기 쯤에는 페르시아, 터키와 북아프리카에 이미 들어와 있었다. 커피에 대한 처음 반응은 그다지 좋지 않았다. 1511년에는 신경을 자극하는 성질 때문에 메카의 보수적인 이맘에 의해 금지되었다. 하지만 이 음료의 인기, 특히 그리스인과 지식인 사이에서의 인기를 꺾을 수 없었고 결국 오스만 투르크 술탄 셀림 1세에 의해 커피 금지령이 폐지되었다. 카이로에서도 비슷한 금지령이 1532년에 세워졌고, 커피샵과 커피 창고들이 파괴되었다. 하지만 이후 1554년 이스탄불에 세계 최초의 커피 가게인 카페 키바 한(Cafe Kiva Han)이 들어서게 된다. 커피는 이슬람 세계에서 유럽으로 퍼졌다. 한 계기는 오스만 제국이 오스트리아의 빈을 점령하면서부터인데 전쟁 상태에서 터키에 머물고 있던 공직자 프란츠 콜스키츠키(Franz Kolschitzky)는 검은 빛깔의 열매를 발견해 들여오게 됐고 1683년에 커피 전문점을 열었다. 지금처럼 커피에 우유를 넣거나 달게 먹는 방식은 오스트리아에서 시작됐다고 한다. 커피는 후에 17세기로 접어들면서 유럽에서 큰 인기를 얻기 시작했다. 유럽으로 커피를 처음 대량 수입하기 시작한 것은 네덜란드 상인이었다. 네덜란드 인들은 자와 섬 지역에 커피 플랜테이션 농장을 지으면서 큰 성공을 거두기도 한다. 10년 동안 중동을 여행한 독일의 의사 레오나르드 라우볼프는 1538년에 커피에 대해 "잉크처럼 검은 음료, 다양한 병, 특히 위에 관련된 질환을 치료하는 데 유용. 이것의 섭취자들은 아침에 돌려쓰는 도자기 잔에서 한 잔씩 마심. 이것은 물과 분누라는 관목에서 나는 열매로 만들어 짐"이라고 적었다. 쉴레이만 아아(프랑스에서는 '솔리만 아가(Soliman Aga)'로 부름)가 1669년 7월 메흐메트 4세의 사절로 베르사유 궁전에서 루이 14세를 접견할 때, 투르크식 커피를 내리는 모습을 선보였고, 이것이 계기가 되어 프랑스 상류층에게는 커피를 담당하는 하인을 고용하는 것이 사회적 지위의 상징이 되었다. 한편, 런던에서는 오스트리아보다도 먼저 커피를 마시고 있었다. 런던 사람들에게 커피숍은 Penny Universities라 불리면서 싼 값에 지식을 공유하고 토론하는 장으로 자리잡았다. 영국인들 사이에서 커피의 인기가 계속 증대됨에 따라 1690년대부터는 미국에도 본격적인 커피 가게 붐이 일어난다. 뉴욕, 보스턴, 필라델피아 등지에서 시작됐으며 1700년이 넘어가면서부터 뉴욕 시에서는 맥주보다 커피가 아침 음료로 선호받게 된다. 사실 커피가 아메리카 대륙의 식민지에 처음 소개되었을 때, 식민지 이주자들은 커피보다 술을 더 즐겨 마셨기 때문에 커피는 별로 인기를 끌지 못했지만 미국 독립 전쟁 중 커피의 수요는 급격히 증가하여, 그러지 않아도 영국 상인의 부재로 공급이 줄어든 커피는 값이 크게 뛰었다. 20세기에 들어서서는 커피 산업 전반에 급진적인 발전이 나타난다. 1900년 힐스 브라더스 사가 진공 포장된 커피 제조에 성공했으며 이듬해에는 일본계 미국인 과학자이던 사토리 카토가 인스턴트 커피를 발명했다. 1938년도에는 네슬레 사 소속 과학자들이 에스프레소 커피 개발에 성공하였으며 1946년에는 아킬레스 가기아(Achilles Gaggia)가 에스프레소 제조기계 발명에 성공하였다. 한국에서의 커피 역사는 대략 1890년 전후로 알려져 있다. 대체적으로 이 시기에 외국의 문물이 많이 들어오던 시기여서 이때 커피가 전파되었다는 다양한 설이 제기되고 있다. 공식문헌상으로는 1895년 을미사변으로 인하여 고종황제가 러시아 공사관에 피신해 있을 때 러시아 공사가 커피를 권했다고 나타나있다. 이렇게 커피를 즐기게 된 고종은 환궁 후에도 커피를 즐겨마시곤 했다고 전해진다. 그리고 이 무렵 서울 중구 정동에 손탁호텔이라는 곳이 세워졌는데 그곳에서는 커피하우스가 있었다. 이것이 최초의 커피하우스였다. 또 이 무렵 일본을 통해서도 커피가 전파되었는데 일본인들이 차린 양식찻집에 의해서 커피가 전파되었다. 그 후 일제강점기 시절 근대적 의미의 다방이 많이 생겨 일본인들이 주로 찾고 몇몇 지식인들과 문학가들이 폭넓게 드나들었다고 한다. 하지만 이러한 다방은 세계2차대전 전후로 하여 대부분 문을 닫았다가 해방과 동시에

미군이 주둔하기 시작하면서 군용식량에 포함되어있던 인스턴트커피는 우리나라 커피문화 발전의 촉매제가 되었다. 그 후 커피믹스가 개발되고, 자판기가 등장하는 등 커피의 대중화를 이루었고 1980년대 이후에는 원두커피 전문점이 등장하고 1999년에는 스타벅스가 국내에 진출하여 이화여대 앞에 1호점을 연것을 기점으로 국내 에스프레소 커피전문점은 폭발적인 성장을 이루게 되었다. 그 이후 더 많은 커피전문점이 들어서면서 커피빈, 파스쿠치, 엔젤리너스, 할리스, 이디야커피, 탐앤탐스 등의 업체들이 치열하게 경쟁을 이루게 되었다. 폭발적인 커피 전문점의 증가로, 현재 서울은 전세계 도시중에서 최고의 밀집도를 보이고 있다.

mage – RAWR Café

Contents_

Café Design 206

Participation Designers 370

Enjoy Coffee2

Coffee Branding & Café Design

0123456789abcdefghijklmnopqrstuvwxyz

Coffee Branding

Designed by ***Studio IeM***

ACC

Archive Coffee Company is a specialty coffee roasting brand. In the past, cafes in Korea mostly focused on the quality of coffee rather than the store experience. These days, however, cafes have gradually evolved as spaces where people communicate, share ideas, and get inspired by each other. Using the repetition and deformation of the basic structure of the letters A and C, our team created visual elements that show the concept of building relationships. This process conveys ACC's vision to become a place where people can share, inspire, and thrive. Moreover, we made three different types of patterns which represent different types of relationships. Those patterns were used in various applications and created a simple and modern aesthetic for the brand.

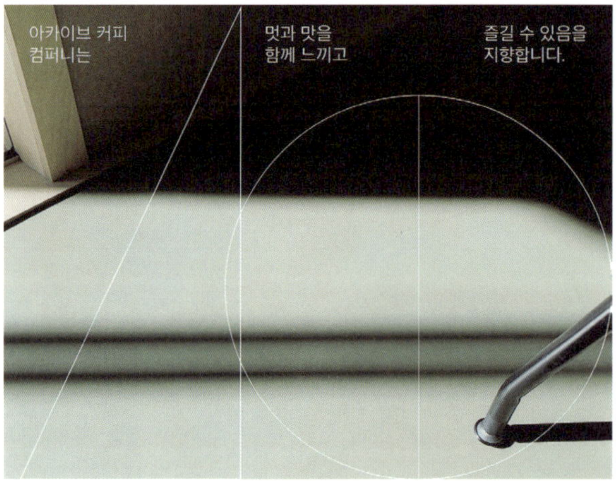

archive
coffee
company

Bar design

컴팩트한 바가 유행인 요즘 카페는
효율적인 바 설계가 중요하다
그만큼 집중되어 있는 공간을 어떻게
구성하고 또 설계하는지에 따라
인건비 운영에도 영향을 줄 수 있다
바리스타로써의 경력 물론 중요하겠지만
카페바를 디자인 설계의 경험의 유무가
바 디자인에 있어서 큰 부분일 것이다
브랜드가 주력하고자 하는 메뉴와 구성
바리스타 구성원과 운영 스타일에 따른
맞추어진 바 디자인은 선택이 아닌
필수로 생각해야 할 것이다.

Barista

모든 운영에 아주 큰 부분을 차지하는 건
사람, 사람운영에는 정해진 답이 없다
숙련 된 바리스타직원으로 구성하여
안정적인 운영과 높은 퀄리티를 지향 할 것이냐
운영이 가벼운 아르바이트로 구성하여
시스템운영을 기초로 효율적인 인건비운영을
할 것이냐에도 선택은 필요하다
브랜드가 지향하고자 하는 컨셉에 맞춘
사람 구성과 교육, 그리고 운영의 시스템화를
통해 운영의 편리와 노무관리까지 어쩌면
그 어떤 무엇보다 중요한 부분일 것 입니다.

Signature

대표하는 시그니쳐 메뉴는
때론 브랜드 보다 더 큰 이슈가 되기도 한다
그 이슈는 사람들로 하여금 발걸음을
옮기게 되는 큰 흡입력을 가지고 있어
매출에 직접적인 연결고리라 볼 수 있다
시즌메뉴와 새로운 메뉴개발에 있어서
소홀히 해서는 안되며 그 작업 자체만으로도
브랜드의 대한 신뢰에 영향을 줄 수 있다
그렇기에 메뉴에 대한 평가와 신뢰는
그 브랜드의 파워와 지속가능성을 보여준다고
판단해도 무리는 아닐 것 이다.

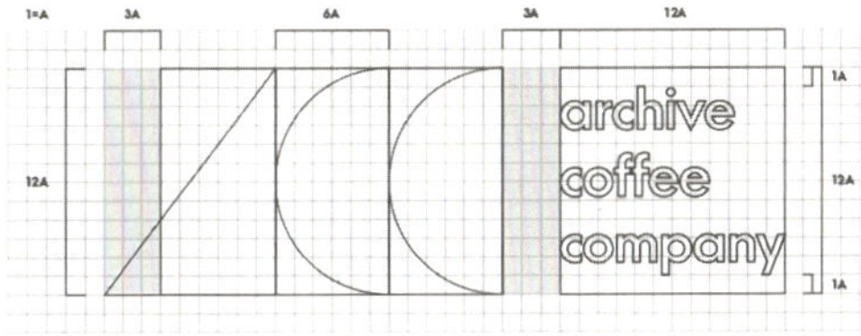
archive
coffee
company

archive
coffee
company

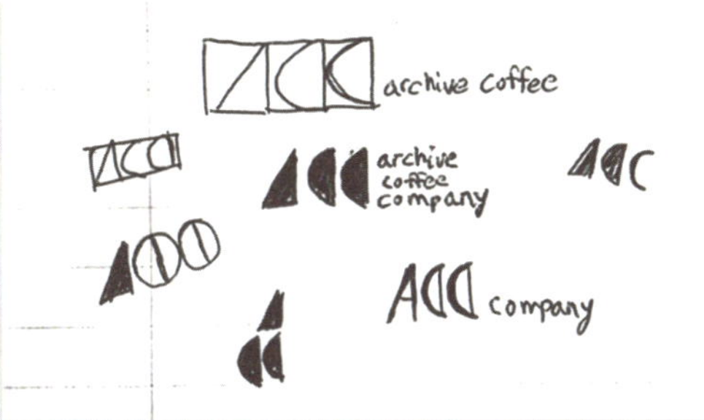
archive coffee
archive
coffee
company
ACC company

archive
coffee
company

archive
coffee
company

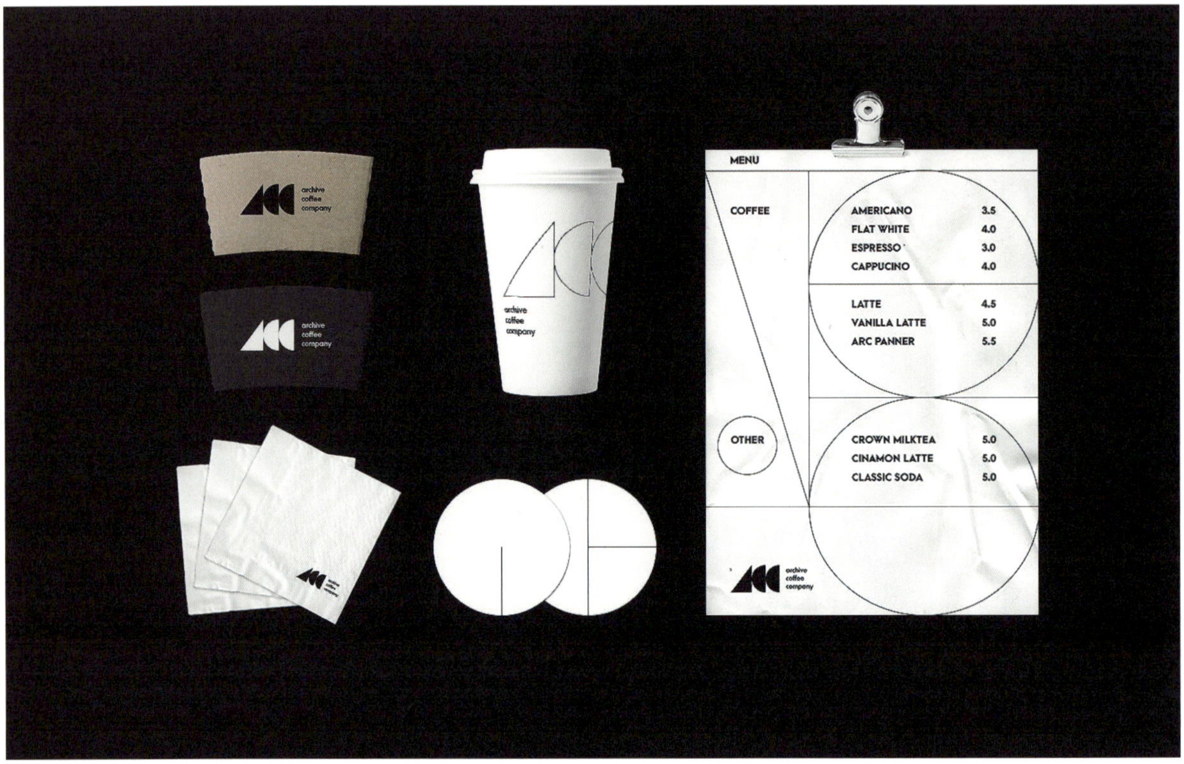
archive
coffee
company
MENU
COFFEE
AMERICANO 3.5
FLAT WHITE 4.0
ESPRESSO 3.0
CAPPUCINO 4.0
LATTE 4.5
VANILLA LATTE 5.0
ARC PANNER 5.5
OTHER
CROWN MILKTEA 5.0
CINAMON LATTE 5.0
CLASSIC SODA 5.0

archive
coffee
company

archive
coffee
company

archive
coffee
company

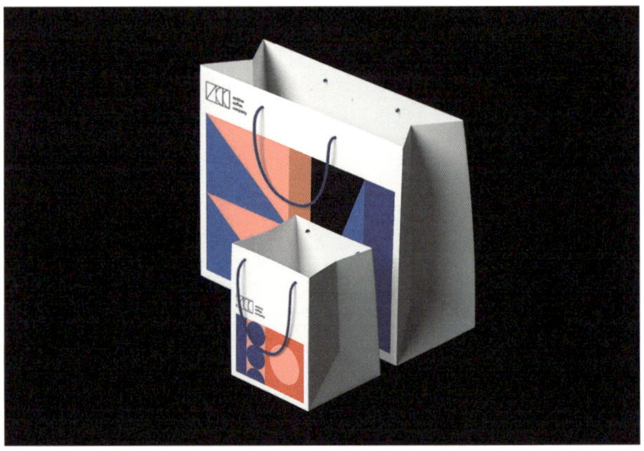

COLOMBIA
archive
coffee
company

archive
coffee
company

archive
coffee
company
Archive Coffee Company
Brand Experience Design
Design by studio leM
2020

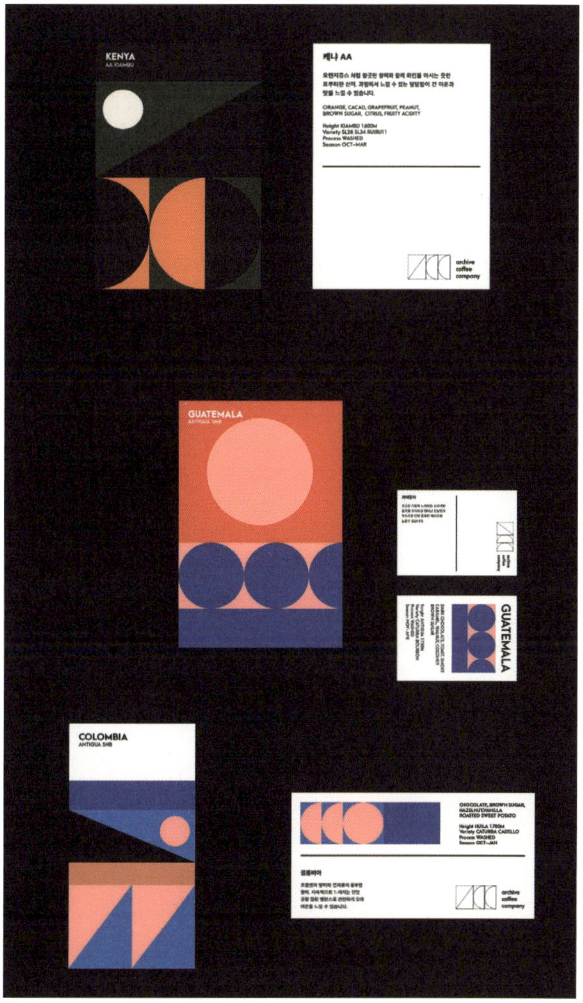
KENYA
AA KIAMBU
케냐 AA
GUATEMALA
GUATEMALA
COLOMBIA
ANTIGUA SHB
archive
coffee
company

KENYA
GUATEMALA
COLOMBIA

archive
coffee
company
archive coffee company

Designed by ***low key Design***

AOKKA

The founder of AOKKA Robin is a doer who loves coffee, feels passionately about outdoors and record. Advocating freedom and romance, willing to share his coffee world. About 10 years ago, he was back to Melbourne, Australia to recording coffee tour with photographer, to let coffee lovers know more about specialty coffee story.

By introducing the aim of the wild club, Aokka relies on the sensual world of coffee to express the pursuit of independence and freedom, the determination and expectation of being adventurous, and face up to the unknown with an outlandish attitude.

COFFEE FOR RAWMANCE is extreme concentration from AOKKA brand concept, In the wilderness, road beacon, tents, horizon etc. We find the wild horizon which belongs to AOKKA, with this concept into a secondary Logo.

COFFEE FOR RAWMANCE, this design concepts to support the entire brand's visual language. Coffee crops grow up in the wilderness around the world, after cultivating,harvesting, processing into green coffee beans. Each sack of green coffee bean though transportation arrives at their destination, and has AOKKA shipping labels and unique sealing rope. We design and use them into exclusive AOKKA's visual language, also for brand packaging system.

RAWMANCE

[rɔ.mæns]

n.romance without processing.

Romance doesn't to be sweet,delicate,perfect,controllable,or it can be natural,the original and free.We born in the wilderness,but free and romantic.

AOKKA
COFFEE
FOR RAWMANCE
AOKKA
Single Origin

AOKKA
Single Origin
CURIOSITY SERIES
AOKKA
Single Origin
EXPLORATION SERIES
AOKKA
Single Origin
ADVENTURE SERIES

AOKKA
ROAST DATE 2021-01-23
AOKKA
ROAST DATE 2021-01-23

AOKKA
AOKKA
AOKKA

AOKKA

ESPRESSO
ESPRESSO
ESPRESSO
COFFEE
FOR RAW
AOKKA
AOKKA
THOR

Rawmance. Coffee for

AOKKA

Coffee for Rawmance.

Coffee for Rawmance.

AOKKA

MAHLKÖNIG

AOKKA
Single Origin
AOKKA
Single Origin
AOKKA

AOKKA
Single Origin
AOKKA
Single Origin
Curiosity Series
AOKKA
Single Origin

AOKKA
125g
EXPLORATION

AOKKA
OKKA
Single Origin

AOKKA
Packing List
By introducing the aim of the Wild Club, AOKKA relies on the Sensual World of Coffee to express the pursuit of independence and freedom, the determination and expectation of being adventurous, and face up to the unknown with an outlandish attitude.
AOKKA

AOKKA
Club, AOKKA relies on the Sensual World of Coffee to express the pursuit of independence and freedom, the determination and expectation of being adventurous, and face up to the unknown with an outlandish attitude.
AOKKA

AOKKA
Single Origin
S
M
This way up
Keep dry
AOKKA
Single Origin

AOKKA
S
AOKKA
M
AOKKA

AOKKA

AOKKA
AOKKA
AOKKA

AOKKA
AOKKA

AOKKA
AOKKA
AOKKA

COFFEE FOR RAWMANCE.

AOKKA
AOKKA
AOKKA
AOKKA
COFFEE FOR RAWMANCE.

AOKKA

ESPRESSO
COFFEE 生于旷野，自由浪漫。
FOR RAWMANCE.
AOKKA

ESPRESSO
AOKKA
ESPRESSO
AOKKA

AOKKA

AOKKA
AOKKA
AOKKA

AOKKA
COFFEE 生于旷野，自由浪漫。
FOR RAWMANCE.
AOKKA

AOKKA
AOKKA
COFFEE 生于旷野，自由浪漫。
FOR RAWMANCE.
AOKKA

Designed by ***Uido Design Studio***

Coffee cups

These cups are made of ceramic, using a production technique called slip casting. Its removable cork grip prevents hand contact with the hot ceramic surface when you're drinking your coffee. They come in two sizes, the 200ml classic cup and the 80ml espresso. The cups began by being produced manually in the Uido's workshop. Now the cups are being produced industrially.

The project was born on Instagram and it aimed to be designed based on people's comments. We made surveys through Instagram stories, giving the community the liberty of choosing different morphological and technological alternatives for the cups. Based on the responses, we followed a path and started the production.

The production process starts with the realization of the model and then make the plaster molds. Once the molds are finished, the slip is carried out so that after a certain time the mold is emptied leaving the piece with the desired thickness. The process ends in the oven, where the first baking is done, then the pieces are glazed and they are baked again.

Six months after the artisanal production, we manufactured the products in China for Empire Coffee. We made small changes in dimensions and angles and we improved the finish of the cork grip. This is the final result of the cups:

Designer : Lautaro Lucero

Design studio : Uido Design Studio LLC

Coffee Cup
How to Use

coffee
cup

coffee
cup

*Designed by **krechet studio***

Cruise

Cruise is a place for everyone who loves coffee, travel, new acquaintances and discoveries. Coffee is loved all over the world and we carefully collected special drink recipes wherever we went. Our customers know that the taste is revealed in combinations - that's why our chefs prepare both desserts and snacks exactly as they do in different parts of the world. A font logo and a complete set of visual identity were developed for the coffee shop: starting from employee badges and stickers on packs of coffee beans, ending with posters and Instagram visual. The corporate identity supports the idea of a cafe: there are no boundaries for pleasure. The color palette of the project is dictated by the variety of desserts that are so fond of complementing a cup of invigorating drink.

Art-director : Tatyana Kirichenko
Designer : Tatyana Toporova

BLEND № 14
РЕЖИМ
РАБО
ТЫ
ШОРТКЕЙК
CRUISE
NO BORDERS
CRUISE
TASTE THE
WORLD
IN
YOUR CUP

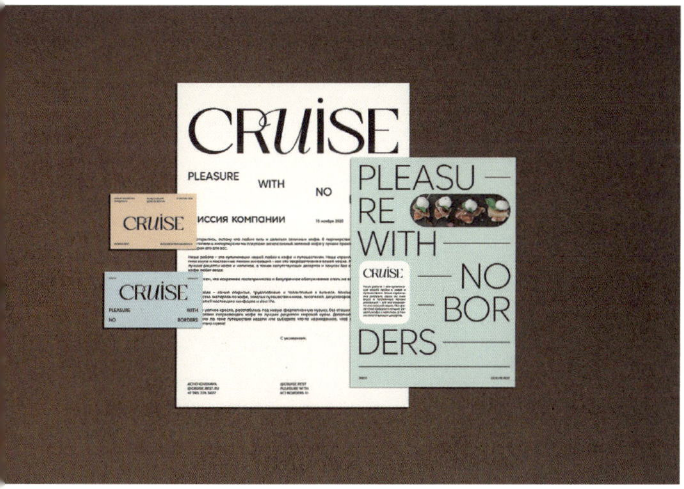
CRUISE
PLEASURE WITH NO
CRUISE
CRUISE
PLEASU
RE
WITH
NO
BOR
DERS
CRUISE

CRUISE
PLEASURE
WITH
NO
BORDERS
CRUISE
CRUISE
CRUISE
PLEASURE
WITH
NO
BORDERS
CRUISE

CRUISE

PLEASURE
WITH
NO
BORDERS
CRUISE

NO BORDERS
CRUISE

РЕЖИМ
РАБО
ТЫ
ПН ЧТ
10:00 24:00
ЧТ ВС
10:00 02:00

TASTE THE WORLD IN YOUR CUP

CRUISE

ШОРТКЕЙК
140 г
305 ₽

TASTE THE WORLD IN YOUR CUP
CRUISE
BLEND № 09

BLEND № 14

CRUISE
PLEASURE WITH NO BORDERS
РЕЖИМ РАБО ТЫ

CRUISE

Designed by ***low key Design***

CUBIC3

Concept :$(m)^3$ as a logo symbolizes individuals, and the gathering of individuals will become a bigger group, namely, "smallness gathers to highlight the power of masses". The fusion of multiple individuals indicates $(m)^3$'s brand concept of being inclusive and collective. $(m)^3$ has been exploring the trend of specialty coffee in life, and it aims to be a specialty coffee brand that can be shared by all.

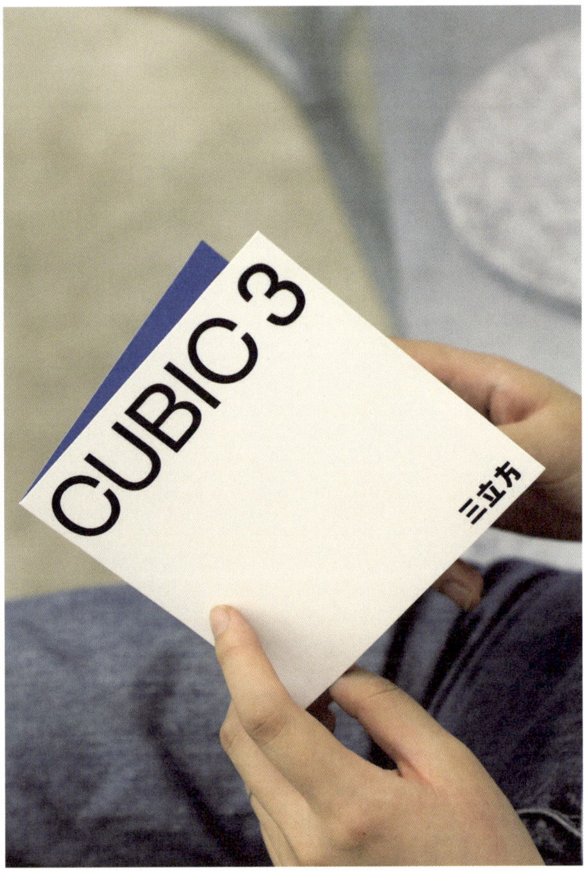

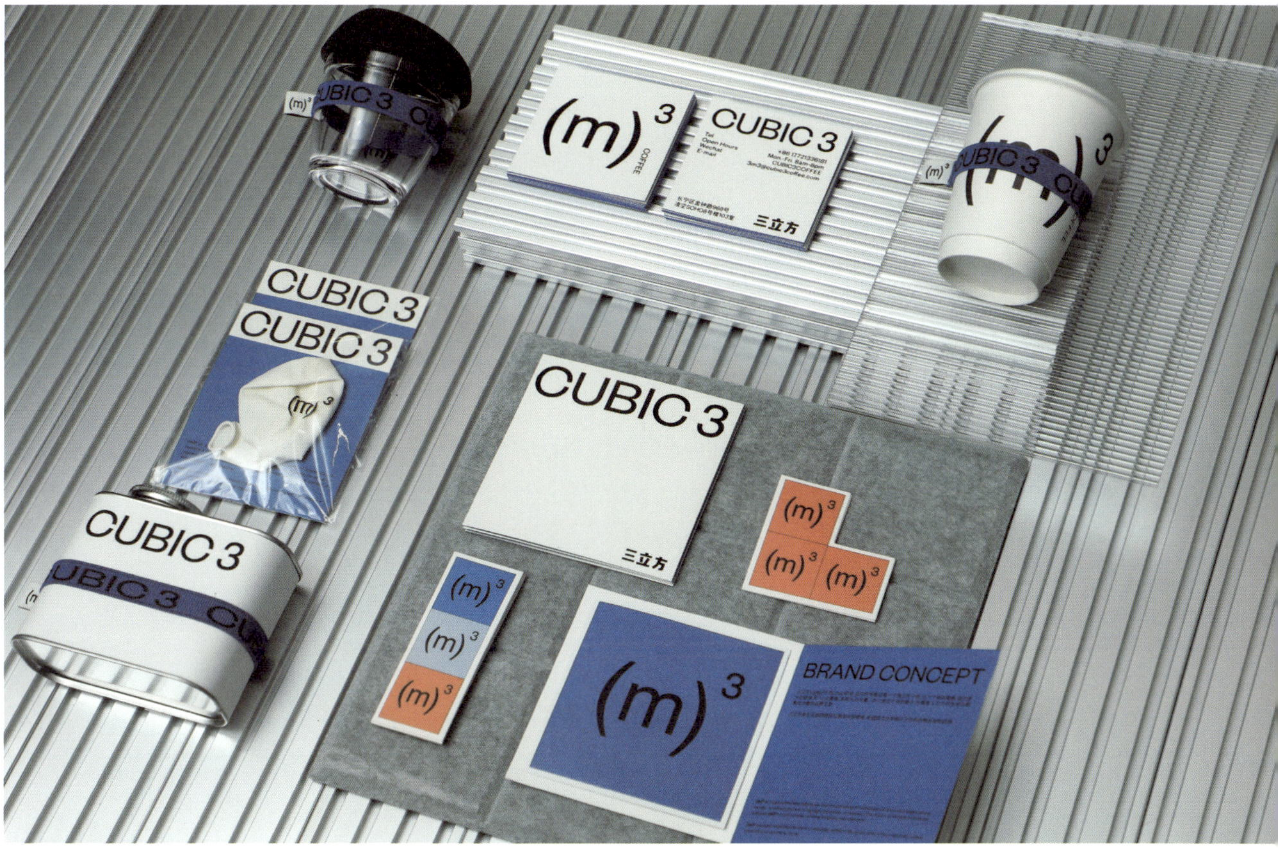
(m)³
COFFEE
CUBIC 3
三立方
BRAND CONCEPT

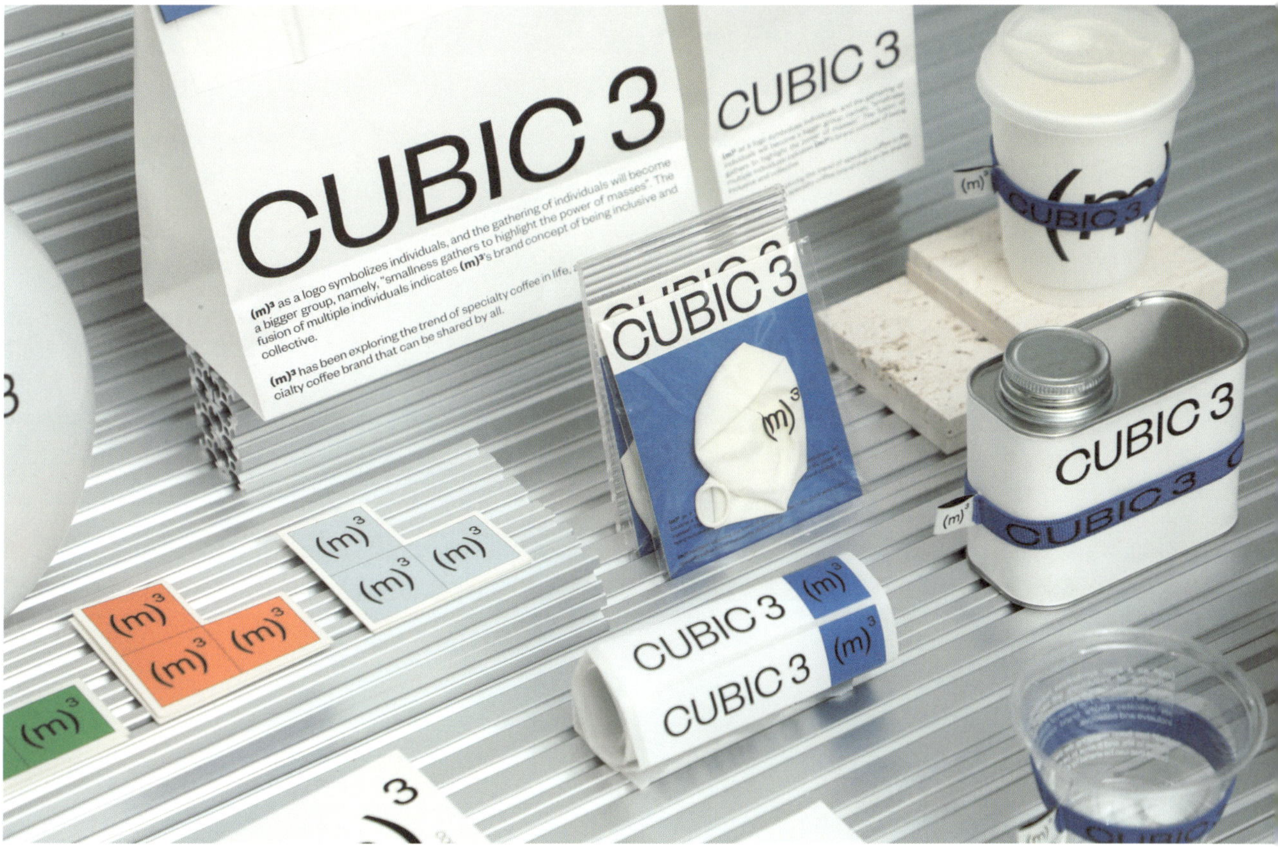
CUBIC 3
(m)³ as a logo symbolizes individuals, and the gathering of individuals will become a bigger group, namely, "smallness gathers to highlight the power of masses". The fusion of multiple individuals indicates (m)³'s brand concept of being inclusive and collective.
(m)³ has been exploring the trend of specialty coffee in life,
cialty coffee brand that can be shared by all.
CUBIC 3
(m)³

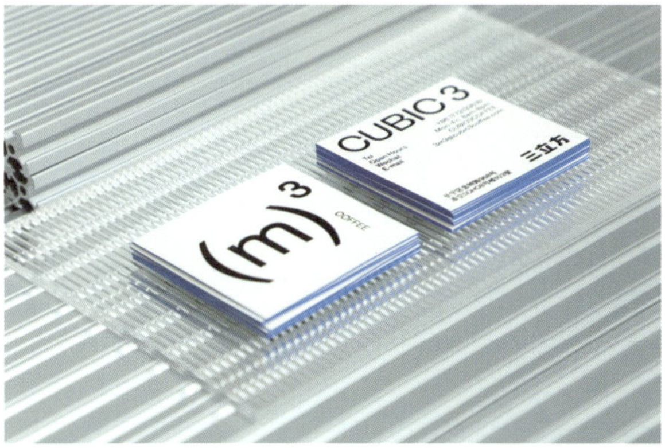
CUBIC 3
(m)3
三立方

三立方

CUBIC 3
(m)3

BRAND CONCEPT
(m)3
(m)3
CUBIC 3
三立方

CUBIC 3
CUBIC 3
(m)3

(m)3

(m)3
CUBIC 3

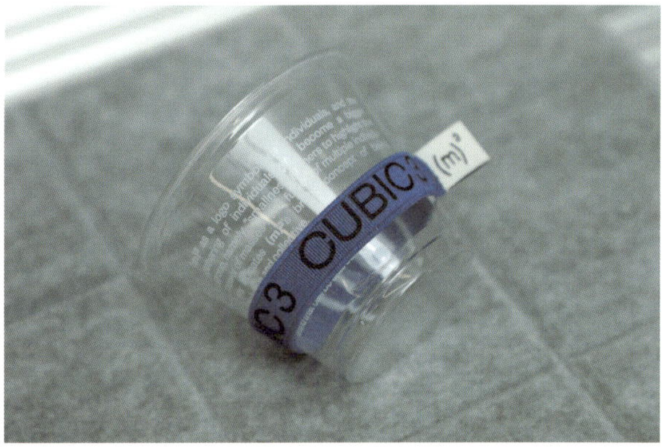
C3 CUBIC3
(m)3

(m)3

(m)3

CUBIC 3

CUBIC 3
(m)3

(m)3

(m)3
(m)3
(m)3
CUBIC 3
CUBIC 3
(m)3

(m)3
(m)3

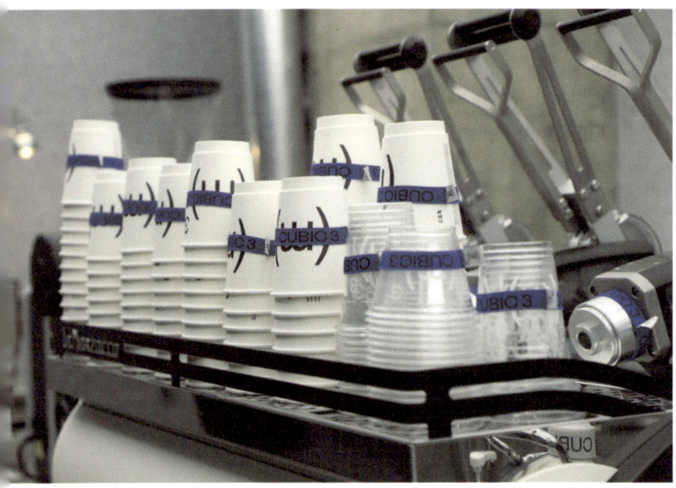
CUBIC 3

LEVA

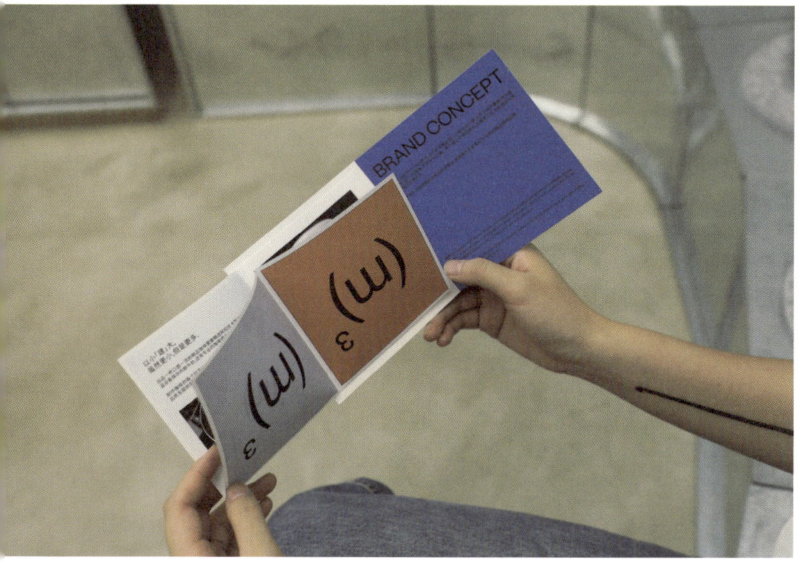
BRAND CONCEPT
(m)³
(m)³

CUBIC 3
(m)³

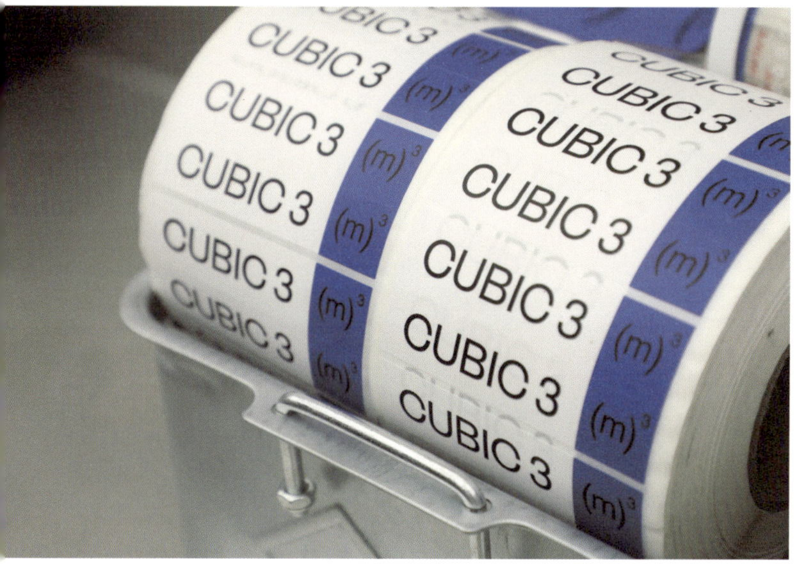
CUBIC 3
(m)³

(m)³
CUBIC 3

(m)³

Designed by ***krechet studio***

Danisant

This is a place where you do not want to rush anywhere, you just want to drink coffee, enjoy the moment, talk with a sincere friend/write letters/fill out a diary/read a book or do nothing at all. This is a place where there is always sunlight, a lot of air and space, simple typography combined with neat drawings/inscriptions. This is a place where you can take a piece of this atmosphere with you in the form of a product: a bag or jam. This is a place where there is communication with visitors through inscriptions: in front of the entrance/on the Cup/on the wall. it's like a good morning message to you, that there's no hurry, everything's fine, you can be yourself. Meaning of the name: coffee with a good person on a sunny day, where the good person is you.

Art-director : Tatyana Kirichenko
Designer : Liza Ulyanova

danisánt

Masculin Féminin

Masculin Féminin
A FILM BY JEAN-LUC GODARD
HERE COMES THE MOVIE

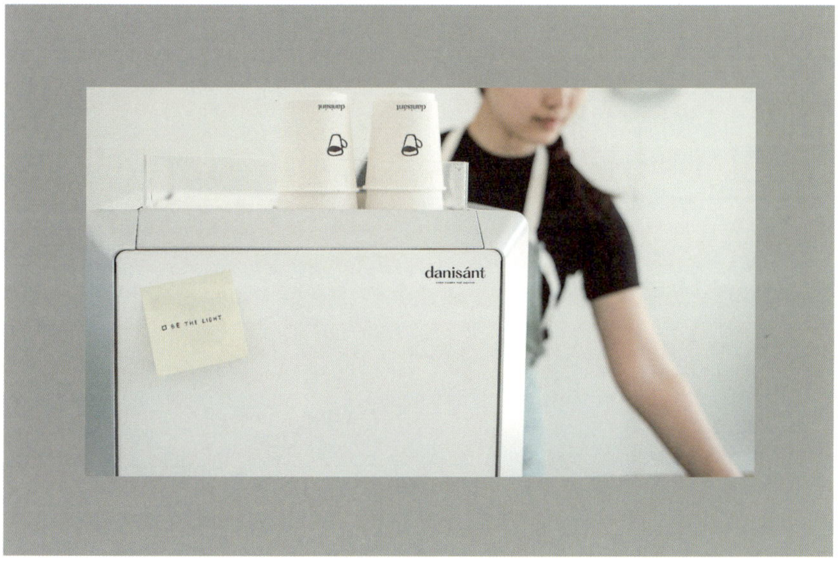
danisánt

danisánt
HERE COMES THE COFFEE

danisánt
danisánt

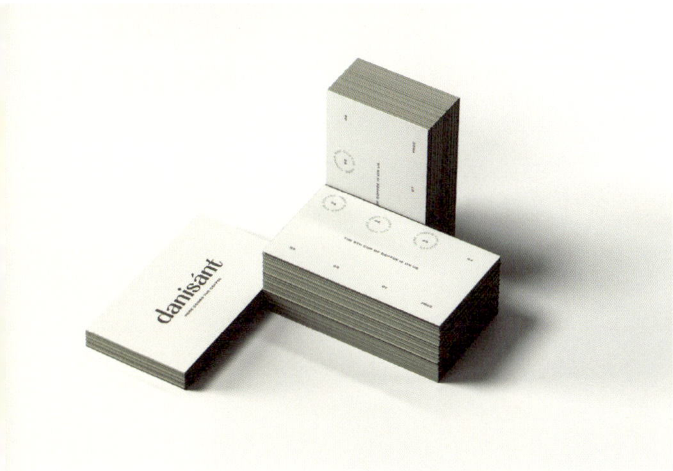
danisánt

danisánt

TAKE YOUR TIME
BE THE LIGHT
danisánt

HERE COME THE DRINKS

Designed by ***Marka Works***

Drop Co

The Client

Drop Co. is a product designed by us to represent a coffee brand.

The Objective

The only thing we aimed at while creating Drop Co. was to reflect whatever we wanted to find in a coffee, into the design.

The Solution

We prepared a colorful and modern design for Drop Co.'s look. We also used the drop icon that we used in the logo design and secondary mark designs that we prepared, in order to have a more remarkable look and feel. In product packaging designs, we chose a different color for each different flavor and we designed them in this way. In addition, we present all our works on our website. so that you can examine our energetic poster designs and our creative slogans on these as well. We hope you like it!

PROUDLY
ROASTED IN
BALTIMORE MA

DROP Co
DC
COFFEE ROASTERS
BALTIMORE MD

DROP CO

DROP CO
Coffee Roasters
CITRUS

DROP CO
Cold Brew
BREWED ON
03/4

DROP CO
Coffee Roasters
KOLA NUTS

DROP CO
Coffee Roasters
KOLA NUTS
DROP CO
Coffee Roasters
CITRUS
DROP CO
Coffee Roasters
COCOA

DROP Co
PROUDLY
ROASTED IN
BALTIMORE MA

PROUDLY
ROASTED IN
BALTIMORE MA
IT'S A
WONDERFUL
LIFE
AFTER
COFFEE
COFFEE ROASTERS
NOUN
COFFEEGASM

ACIDITY NOTES
BODY NOTES
FINISH NOTES
AROMA NOTES

DROP Co
CITRUS
ACIDITY NOTES
BODY NOTES
FINISH NOTES
AROMA NOTES
PROUDLY
ROASTED IN
BALTIMORE MA
EXPLORE

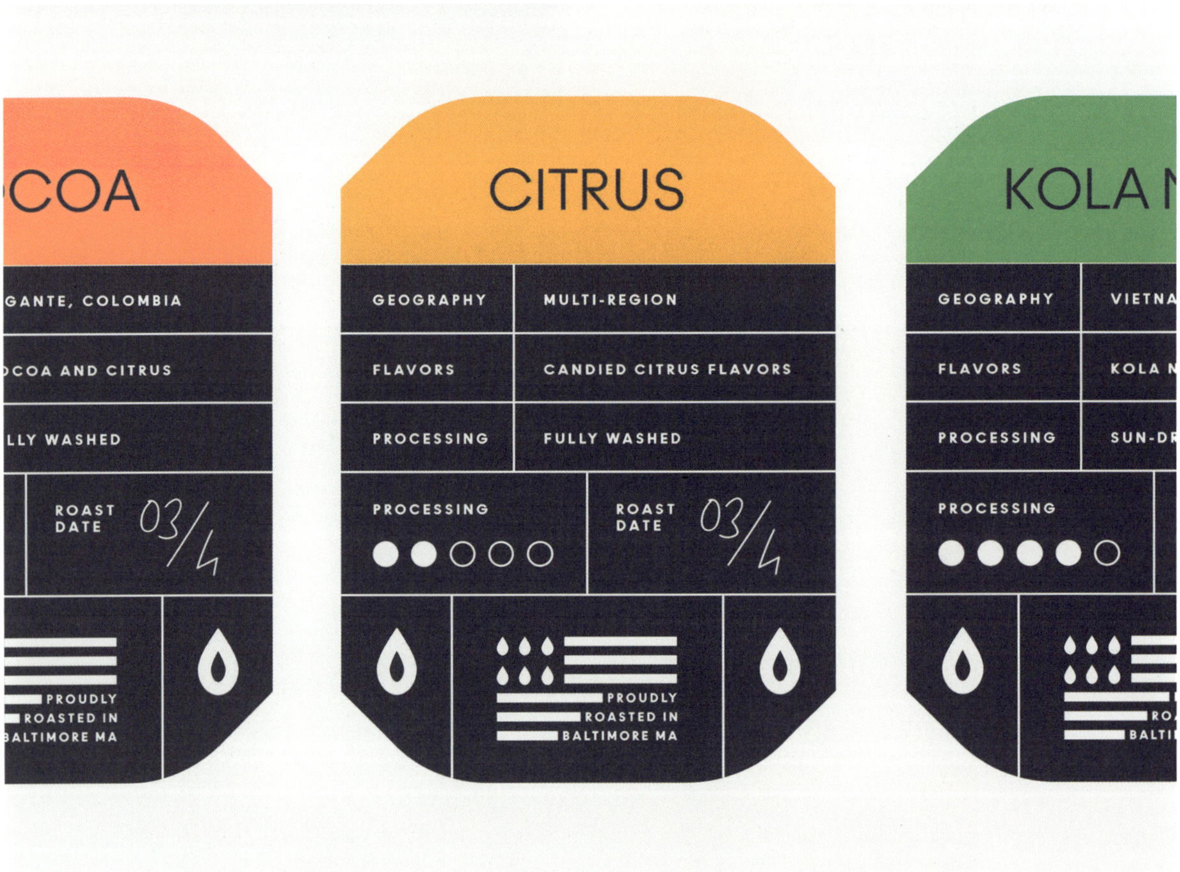
COA
GANTE, COLOMBIA
COA AND CITRUS
LLY WASHED
ROAST
DATE
03/4
PROUDLY
ROASTED IN
BALTIMORE MA
CITRUS
GEOGRAPHY
MULTI-REGION
FLAVORS
CANDIED CITRUS FLAVORS
PROCESSING
FULLY WASHED
PROCESSING
ROAST
DATE
03/4
PROUDLY
ROASTED IN
BALTIMORE MA
KOLA
GEOGRAPHY
VIETNA
FLAVORS
KOLA N
PROCESSING
SUN-DR
PROCESSING

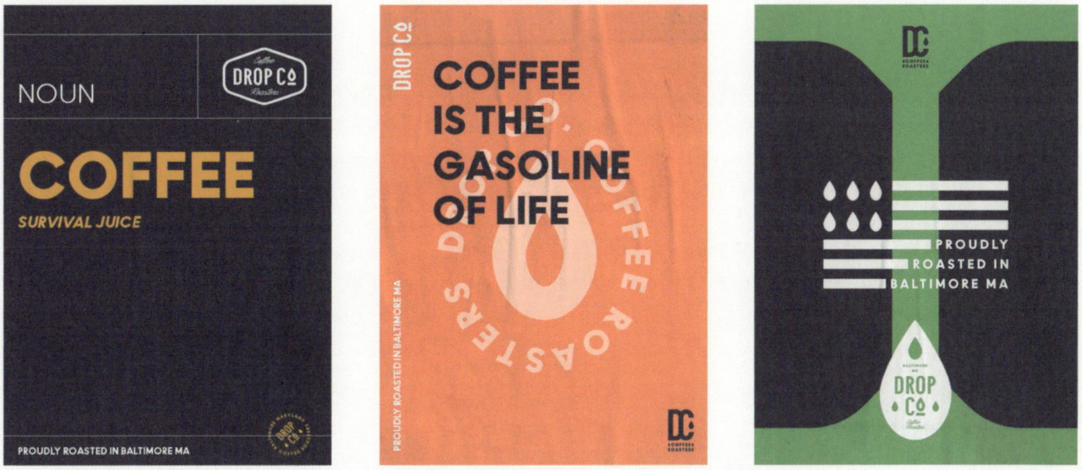
NOUN
DROP Co
COFFEE
SURVIVAL JUICE
PROUDLY ROASTED IN BALTIMORE MA
DROP Co
COFFEE
IS THE
GASOLINE
OF LIFE
DROP CO. COFFEE ROASTERS
PROUDLY ROASTED IN BALTIMORE MA
DC
PROUDLY
ROASTED IN
BALTIMORE MA
DROP
Co

NOUN
COFFE
SURVIVAL JUICE
PROUDLY ROASTED IN BALTIMORE MA
OFFEE
THE
ASOLINE
F LIFE
DC
PROUDLY
ROASTED IN
BALTIMORE MA
DROP
Co

Designed by ***Uido Design Studio***

Empire Coffee

Case study of all the work made for the client Empire Coffee from Qatar. Brand Identity, Graphic Design, Product Design, Interior Design, Illustrations and Sound Design made by Uido Design Studio in 2020-21.

THE BRIEF

Redefining their story. Empire Coffee was an already well positioned speciality coffee brand from Doha, Qatar. But they didn't have a strong brand identity that could express its true personality and that's why they reached out to us.

With the Qatari culture in mind and having the coffee transportation dhow as the most recognisable element, we made a bold and authentic brand with a creative and artistic identity.

After that we designed all the packaging, graphics and illustrations along with both industrial and hand-made products and even the interior design for their two stores and the whole company's building with their offices and manufacturing areas.

After developing the new brand identity for Empire Coffee, we started to give it more voice through some characters and illustrations that showed their personality and connected with their clients enhancing their experience.

We come up with a flat style with minimal details and fine lines and that relies in the brand identity concepts and graphic complements. The illustrations had to look similar between them but we let some space to come up with different ideas and details for every illustration to reinforce the creative spirit that the we previously define for the brand.

EMPIRE

EMPIRE
COFFEE

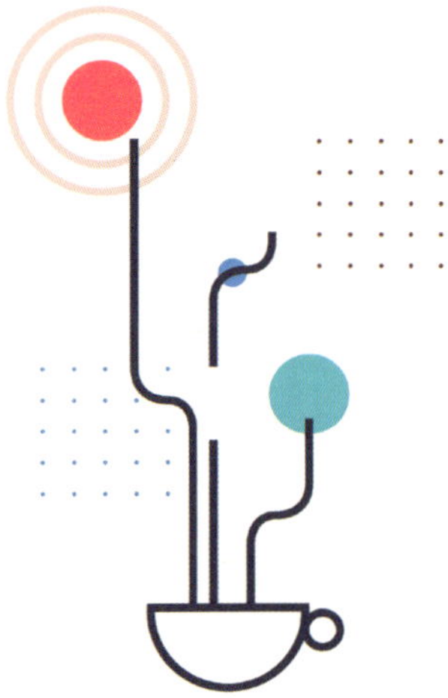

EMPIRE
COFFEE

LOVE IS IN THE AIR
AND
SMELLS LIKE
COFFEE

Life is
better
with
coffee

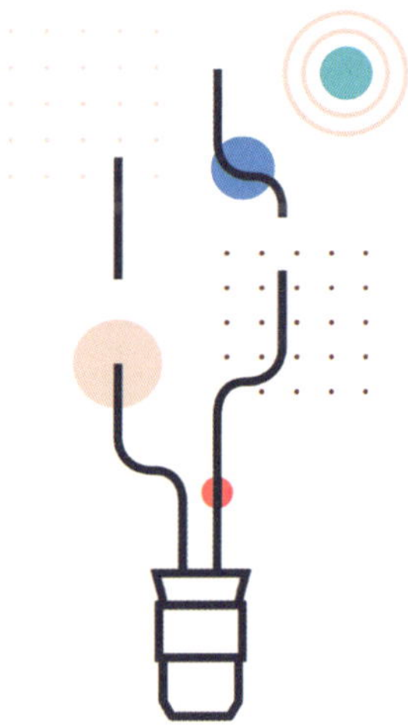

Ethiopia
يبويثا
Variety characteristics
خصائص متنوعة
Aroma
قحذار
Acidity
قضومحه
Sweetness
ةولاح
Body
ةماو
Aftertaste
قاذم

Variety Information
Ethiopia - Guji Shakiso
Filter
Honey
1800 - 2110 MASL
أثيوبيا - غوجي شاكيسو
منقى
عسل
1800 - 2110 MASL
Notes
Berries aroma with a taste of honey mixed with the acid notes of lemon and apple with dark chocolate finish.

EMPIRE
Coffee
EMPIRE
Crafted Speciality Coffee

EMPIRE
empirecof
Doha, State of Qatar
EMPIRE

EMPIRE
Drip bag
5
Drip bags
empirecof.qa

EMPIRE
COFFEE

EMPIRE
Coffee
EMPIRE
Coffee
EMPIRE

EMPIRE

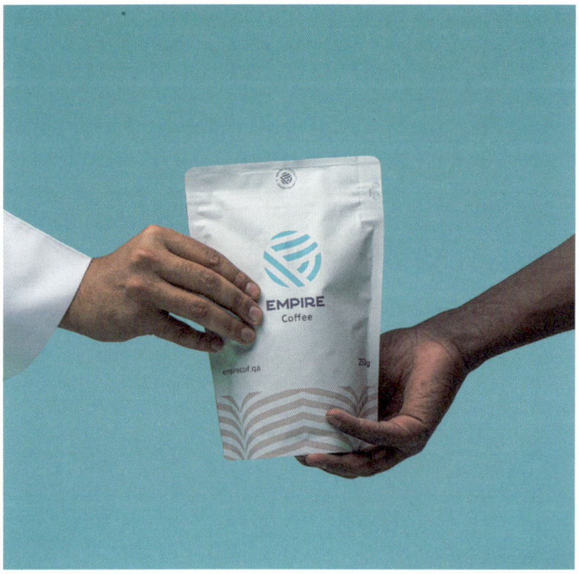
EMPIRE
Coffee

EMPIRE
COFFEE

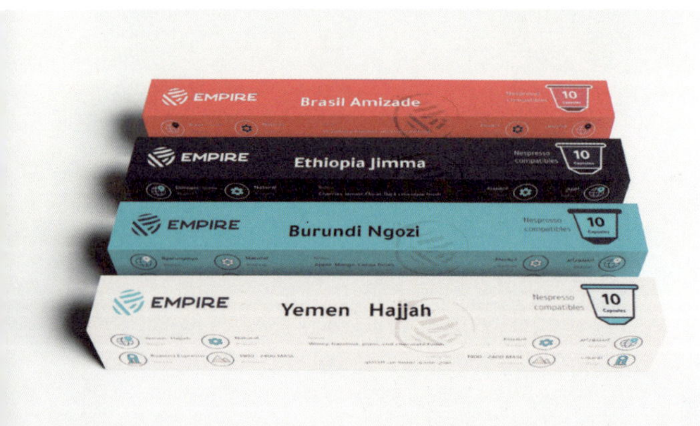
EMPIRE
Brasil Amizade
10
EMPIRE
Ethiopia Jimma
10
EMPIRE
Burundi Ngozi
10
EMPIRE
Yemen Hajjah
10

EMPIRE • SPECIALITY CRAFTED COFFEE

Life is better with coffee
EMPIRE

EMPIRE
Drip bag
5

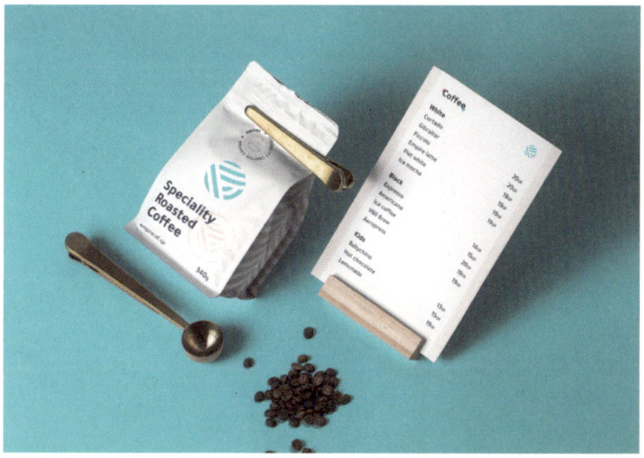
Speciality Roasted Coffee

EMPIRE

EMPIRE COFFEE

EMPIRE
Coffee
empirecof.qa
250g

Designed by ***Serena Studio***

GOODNEWS™

Good News was born as a response to the pandemic with the mission to generate good vibes and create moments of happiness in the neighbourhoods where they are located. Created by three young, talented and ingenious entrepreneurs, who revolutionised the kiosks and transformed them into modern and cool environments, while preserving the essence and tradition. Its clean and minimalist design gives the brand values such as proximity, modernity and flavour, reflected in its packaging, cups, bags and printed pieces. Good News, wants to be part of everyone, the meeting point, the best coffee kiosk and undoubtedly the best stock of magazines and newspapers.

Credits: Carla Serena, Jose Aponte, Jaume Portella, Ángel Ruíz

RAMBLA
DE
CATALUNYA
Good Coffee
GoodNews
GoodNews
GoodNews

jura
Good News
Good News

Good News
Good News

GOOD COFFEE FOR GOOD PEOPLE

GoodNews™
GoodNews
GoodNews
BARCELONA
DECAF

GoodNews™
CUENTERETE
ANTIGUA, GUATEMALA

Designed by ***Studio IeM***

Keungkeung / 킁킁

Keungkeung, or Sniff Sniff, is a mimetic word that describes the sound of sensing the smell of freshly baked goods. We selected this name because smell is one of the strongest senses that attracts people. Keungkeung's logotype was developed based on the shape of the Korean word '□□' which is consisted of the most basic components: straight lines and circles. By using the characteristics of consonants and vowels of Hangul, we created the logotype visually harmonious yet experimental. Furthermore, we completed the full identity by setting bright yellow as the main color to create a positive and fresh image.

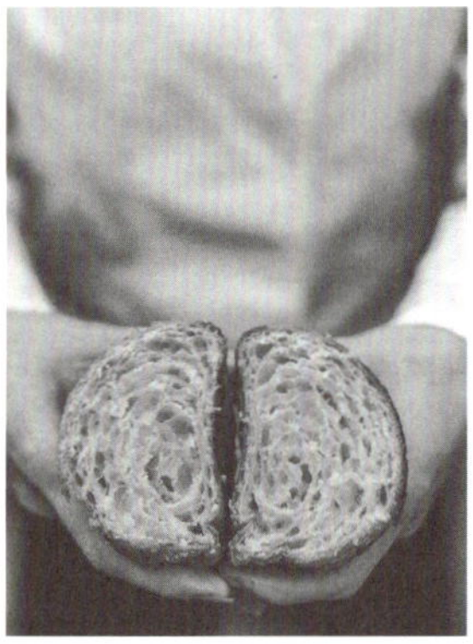

brand story

"킁킁" 어디서 나는 냄새지?
어디서부터인지 모를
길 잃은 내 발걸음은 그 냄새로
부터 시작 된 거 같다

맛있는 냄새는 본능적으로 사람을
끌어들이는 마법과 같은 능력이 있습니다
그렇게 발걸음을 이끌려 온 이 곳에서
행복함을 만날 수 있길 바라는 마음으로
브랜드를 만들었습니다.

ㅋㅡㅇ ㅋㅡㅇ

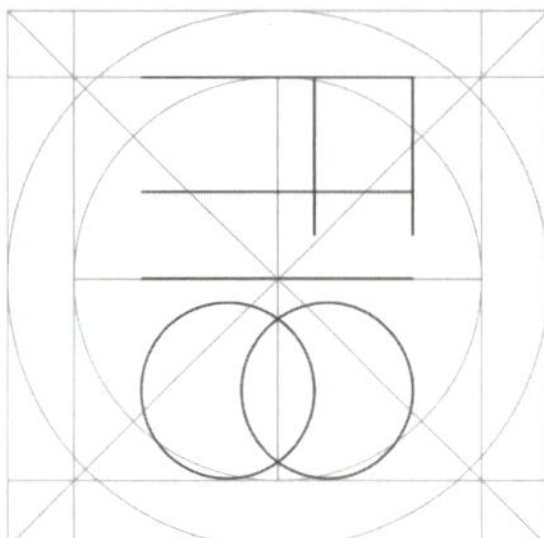

14pt FRESH MADE ODOR
18pt FRESH MADE ODOR
24pt FRESH MADE ODOR
30pt FRESH MADE ODOR
38pt FRESH MADE ODOR
48pt FRESH MADE ODOR

logosystem

킁킁의 브랜드아이덴티티는 직선과 원형만을 이용해 글자를 개발한 후 직선을 기초로 변형과 반복을 통해 로고에 적용했습니다. 한글이 가지고 있는 기하학적 요소를 최대 활용하여 현대적인 느낌을 주었으며, 라이트 한 직선의 글자 형태로 가독성을 높여 대중적인 접근을 유도하였습니다.

Baguette
Campagne
EGGTART
FRESH
MADE
ODOR
3000WON
COUPON

FRESH
MADE
ODOR

FRESH
MADE
ODOR

FRESH MADE ODOR

Designed by **Marka Works**

Las Habitas

<u>The Client</u>

Las Habitas, is an establishment that has adopted the principle of offering us the most delicious coffee. They opened their first store in İzmir's Bostanlı Region.

<u>The Objective</u>

Las Habitas offers coffee with high quality and innovative techniques while preserving its natural properties. In addition to coffee, they also offer us healthy food and beverage products.

<u>The Solution</u>

We have created a brand identity for them that draws attention with its vintage look and also carries modern traces. We have created modern menu designs, unique coffee packaging designs, hot and cold coffee cup designs, healthy drinks' label designs, coaster designs which are all in accordance with the themes and colors we have chosen during our branding process. In this process, we carefully processed every detail from the font we have usen to the colors we have chosen and presented all to you. We hope you like it!

SPECIALITY COFFEE
DRINK
HOT & COLD
HOMEMADE
BAKERY
ALL DAY BRUNCH
ESTD 2020
LAS HABITAS
Bostanlı

SPACING
LAS HABITAS
LAS HABITAS
LOGO DEVELOPMENT
50 PX
LAS HABITAS
50 PX
LAS HABITAS
35 PX
LAS HABITAS
35 PX
LAS HABITAS
20 PX
LAS HABITAS
20 PX
LAS HABITAS
LAS HABITAS
TONE & MOOD
LAS HABITAS
COLOR GUIDELINES
LAS HABITAS
MOODBOARD
LAS HABITAS
TYPOGRAPHY SELECTION
Habitas Sans Regular
Habitas Sans Regular
abcdefghijklmnopqrstuvwxyz
ABCDEFGHIJKLMNOPQRSTUVWXYZ
1234567890
LAS HABITAS

STRATEGY
LAS HABITAS
LOGO DEVELOPMENT
ESTD 2020
LAS HABITAS
Bostanlı
PRIMARY
SECONDARY
PACKAGING
Las HABITAS
LABELING
LAS HABITAS
COFFEE CO
TONE
ALL DAY BRUNCH

SPECIALITY COFFEE
DRINK
HOT & COLD
HOMEMADE
BAKERY
ALL DAY BRUNCH
LAS HABITAS
Bostanlı

PANTONE
PANTONE
PANTONE
PANTONE
PANTONE

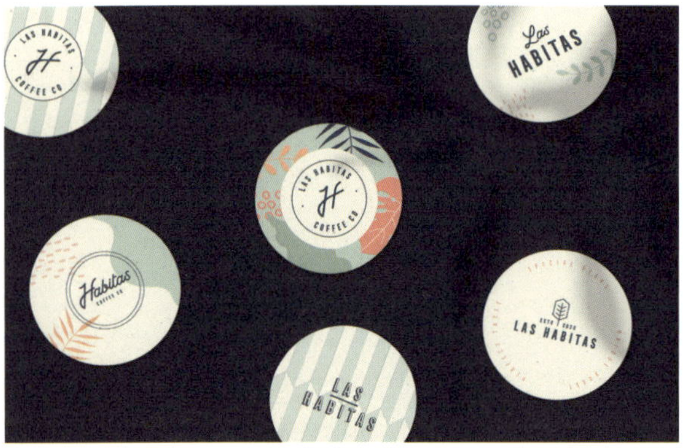
Las
HABITAS
LAS
HABITAS

SOMETHING NEW
Las
HABITAS
MENU
LAS
HABITAS

LAS HABITAS
COFFEE CO

Habitas

Cold Brew

Las
HABITAS

Las
HABITAS
HELLO

Las
HABITAS
COFFEE CO

LAS
HABITAS

Las
HABITAS
COLD
PRESSED
GET WELL

Las
HABITAS
COLD
PRESSED
RELAX

LAS HABITAS

COLD
PRESSED
LAS HABITAS
COFFEE CO

LAS HABITAS
COFFEE CO

HABITAS
COLD
PRESSED

HELLO

Las
HABITAS

SPECIALITY COFFEE
DRINK
HOT & COLD
BAKERY
ALL DAY BRUNCH
EXPERIENCE BAR

EXPERIENCE BAR

COLD
PRESSED

LAS HAB
Bostanlı

Las
HABITAS

LAS HABITAS
COFFEE CO

LAS HABITAS
COFFEE CO

Designed by ***Studio Woork***

Mineral Cafe

Located at Jakarta, Indonesia. Mineral Cafe offers home-made food and beverages at its best and bring out home feels that are comforting, kind to the world, and delicious. They also serve quality coffee, milk tea, chocolate and herbs.

"This old house, like a mineral, is carved out to allow natural light and air to make their way in—breathing another kind of life inside. We removed the ceiling and doors and turned the wood frames into furniture you see around you. We let most things intact: the tacky wall faux-nature in relief? There. Through the process, we asked the house "it was once so tight and dark, are you seeing the sun and breathing safely now?" Imaginarily, of course. Because a house doesn't speak. Or does it? But anyway, it is safe to be here. Let us be inside, along with our plants, the light, the air, and this moment." said Muhammad Kamil (Architect).

Inspired by nature, we designed the brand with an organic approach. The identity is inspired from a mineral stone shape itself. The brand's personality maintains contrasts from shapes, typography, and colors that creates a homey cafe. We also put thought into the logo identity to create a strong image and accentuate the brand, while still giving a casual and welcoming look for the audience.

The concept of 'upcycling' is one of our purpose. So we try to use as much as residual building materials of the cafe to create the environmental signages. Starting from using old metal leftovers and stones, we try to keep in line with the direction and concept.

All the collaterals and packaging for take-away orders are also eco-friendly, it consists of paperbags, meal containers, and plates. The materials used are kraft brown paper, recycled paper, clay and cardboard, complete with the cafe's identity printed on it.

Additional:

We did a thorough research about how minerals are formed. In this case we took an example from salt. Natirum Sodium Chloride (salt) is simply a combination result of a solidification between Natrium and Chloride, which results in NacL. We try to connect the process of the merging between two particles into the idea of a cafe where many individuals can gather into one place, creating a relationship or community.

In Geology and Mineralogy, a mineral or mineral species is, broadly speaking, "a solid chemical compound with a fairly well-defined composition and specific crystal culture, that occurs naturally in pure form". This statement inspired us to come up with the name "Mineral".

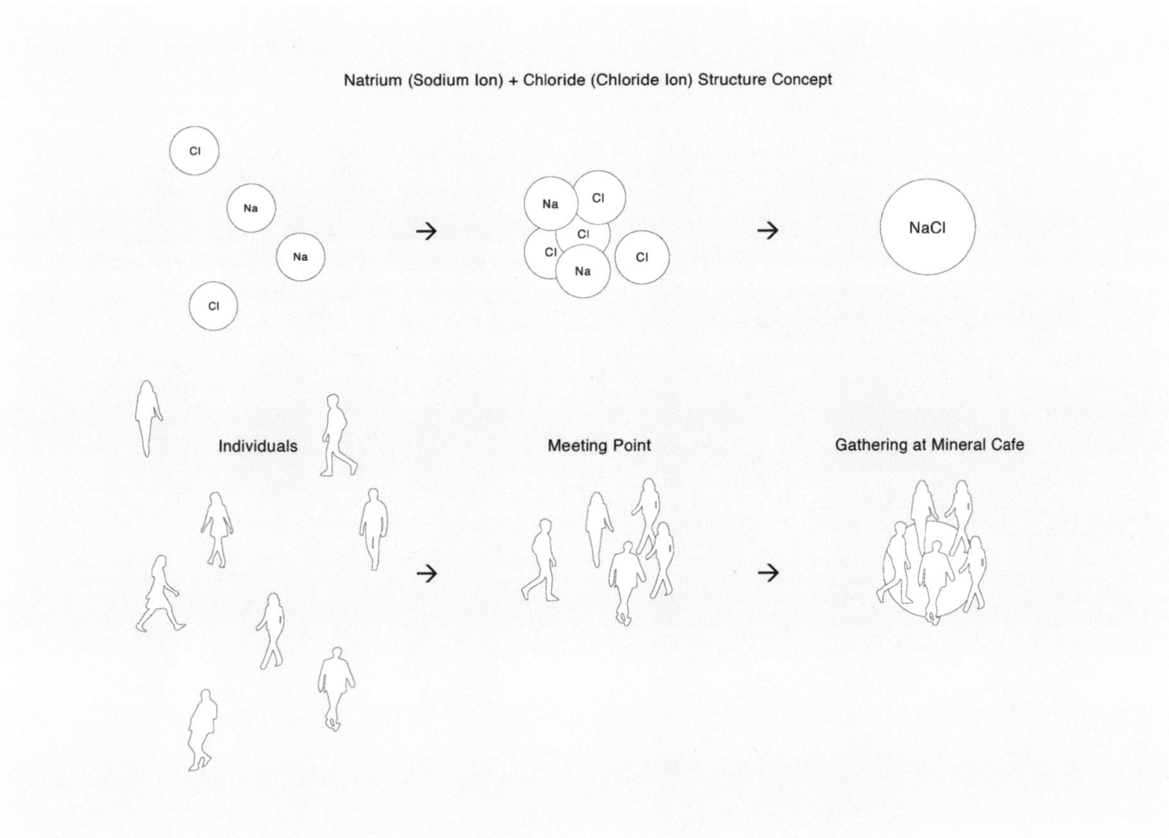

Design Agency: Studio Woork
Design team: Art Director & Designer (Io Woo)
Architect: Studio Ppooll (Muhammad Kamil)
Photography: Studio Woork
Client: Mineral Cafe
Location (complete address): 17, Gandaria Tengah III, South Jakarta, Indonesia, 12130
Finishing materials: Environmentally Friendly Materials

159
5 cm
NS70
N185
lower

mineral

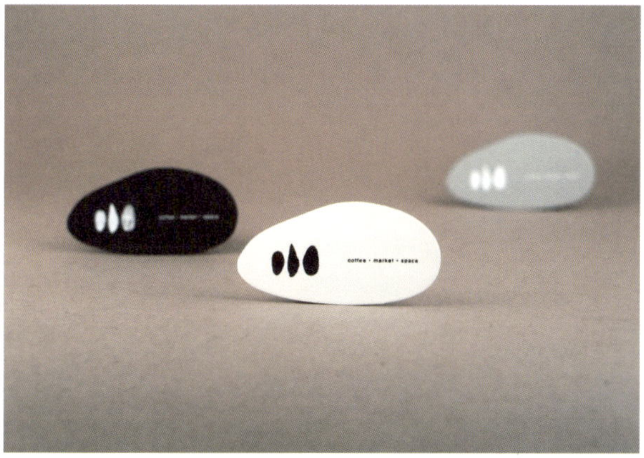

mineral
coffee • market • space

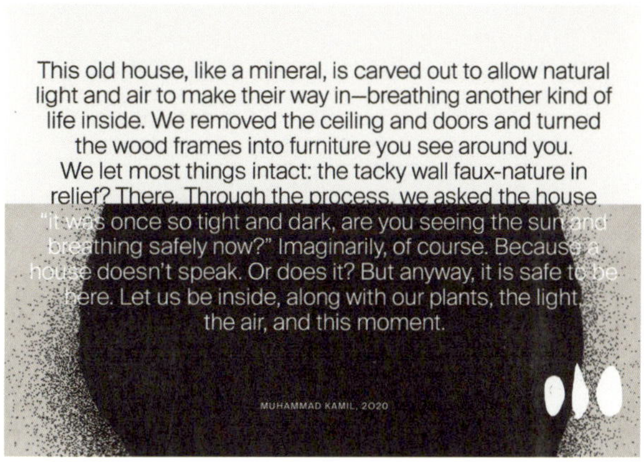
This old house, like a mineral, is carved out to allow natural
light and air to make their way in—breathing another kind of
life inside. We removed the ceiling and doors and turned
the wood frames into furniture you see around you.
We let most things intact: the tacky wall faux-nature in
relief? There. Through the process, we asked the house
"it was once so tight and dark, are you seeing the sun and
breathing safely now?" Imaginarily, of course. Because a
house doesn't speak. Or does it? But anyway, it is safe to be
here. Let us be inside, along with our plants, the light,
the air, and this moment.
MUHAMMAD KAMIL, 2020

coffee • market • space

mineral
coffee • market • space

coffee • market • space

mineral

How to make a 1-Liter SIP (Sub-Irrigated Planter) using Mineral Cafe Plastic Bottle

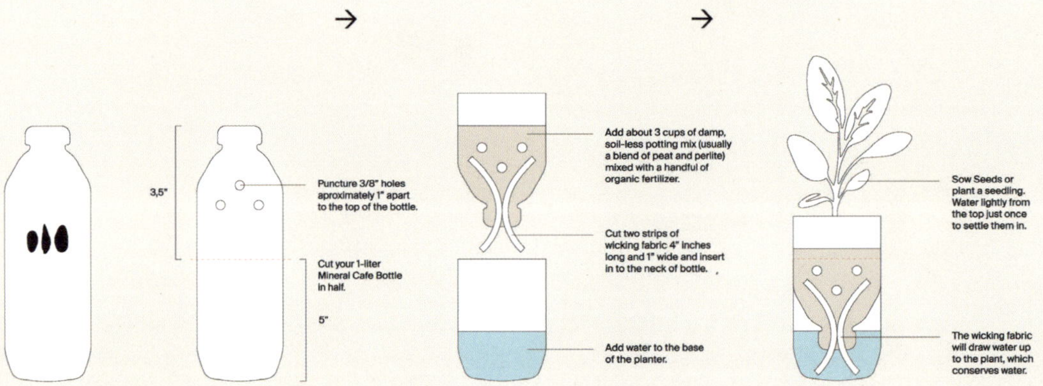

ES KOPI SUSU
EARL GREY COFFEE JELLY
ORIGINAL MILK TEA
JERUK YAKULT
BERAS KENCUR SUSU
EARL GREY MILK TEA
STRAWBERRY YOGHURT
MATCHA MILK TEA

ES KOPI SUSU

BASIC NOTEBOOK
mineral
BASIC NOTEBOOK
mineral
BASIC NOTEBOOK
mineral

mineral

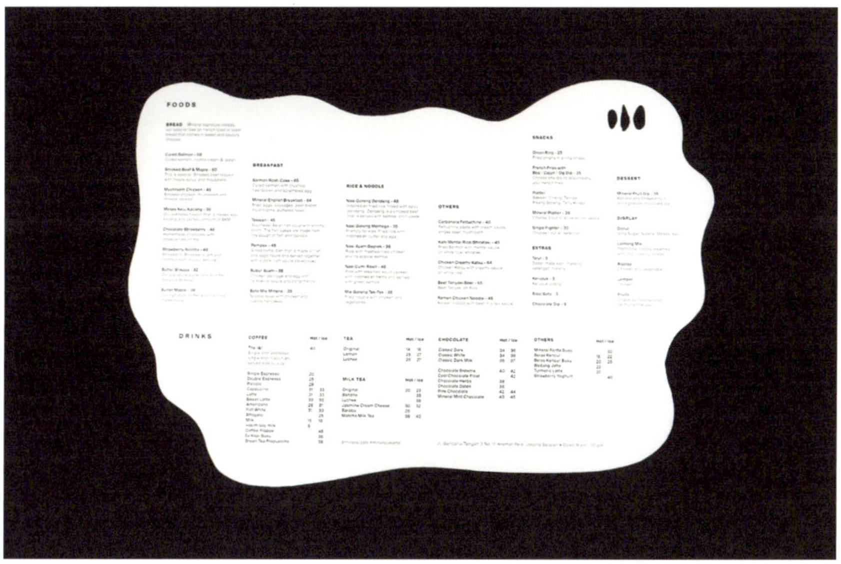
FOODS
DRINKS

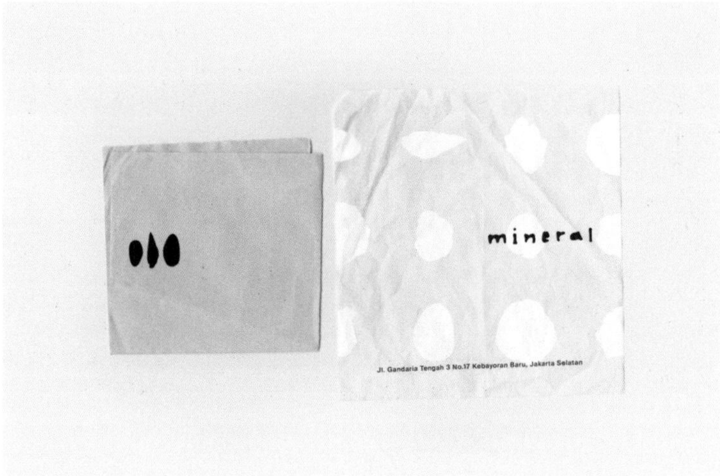
mineral
Jl. Gandaria Tengah 3 No.17 Kebayoran Baru, Jakarta Selatan

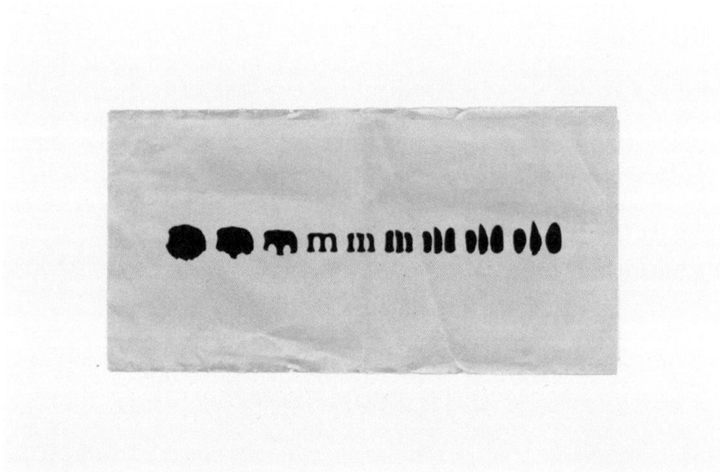

mineral

mineral

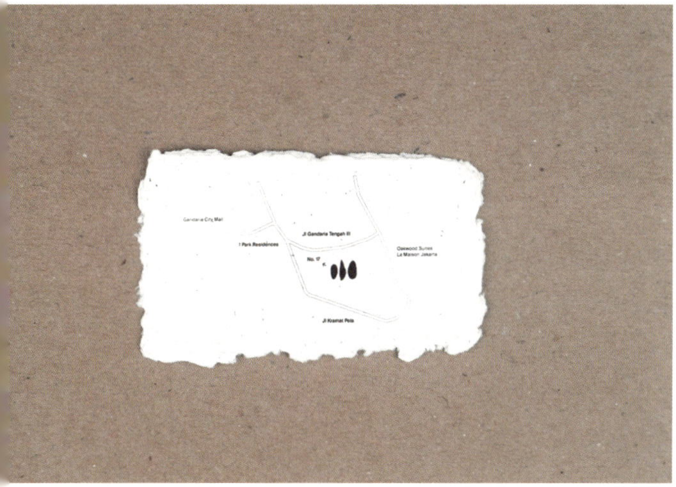
Gandaria City Mall
Jl Gandaria Tengah III
Park Residences
Oakwood Suites
La Maison Jakarta
No. 17
Jl Kramat Pela

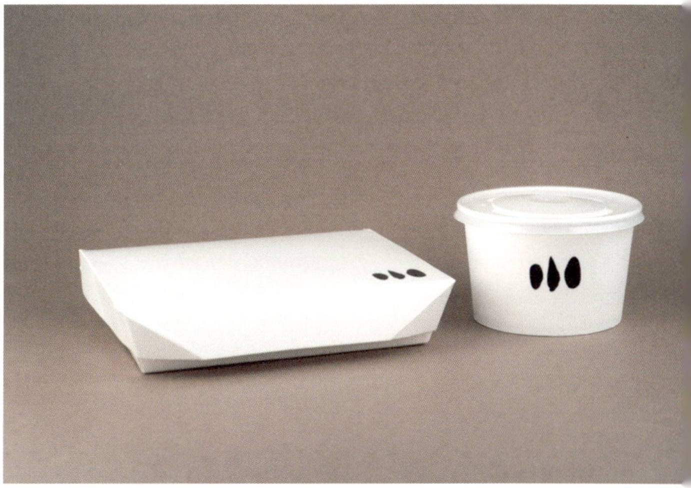

mineral
coffee • market • space

mineral

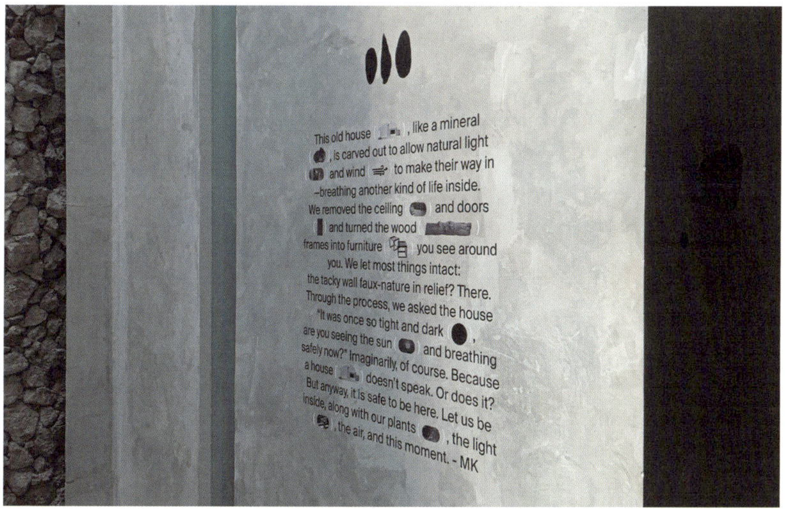
This old house , like a mineral
, is carved out to allow natural light
and wind to make their way in
–breathing another kind of life inside.
We removed the ceiling and doors
and turned the wood
frames into furniture you see around
you. We let most things intact:
the tacky wall faux-nature in relief? There.
Through the process, we asked the house
"It was once so tight and dark ,
are you seeing the sun and breathing
safely now?" Imaginarily, of course. Because
a house doesn't speak. Or does it?
But anyway, it is safe to be here. Let us be
inside, along with our plants , the light
, the air, and this moment. - MK

coffee • market • space

mineral
coffee • market • space

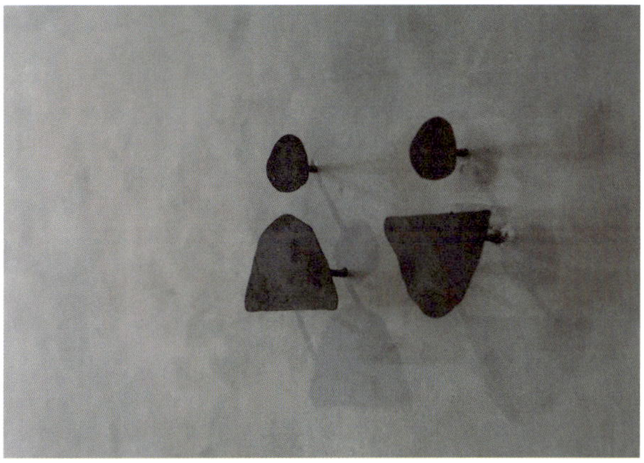

Smoking Area

Prayer Room
Smoking Area
Kitchen
Order Here
Private Room
Staff Only

Designed by **Marka Works**

Music & Beans

<u>The Client</u>

Music & Beans is a coffee shop in London that offers its customers unique coffee and daily fresh bakery with tasty flavors. However, their concept is a little unusual. It allows you to enjoy coffee and music at the same time.

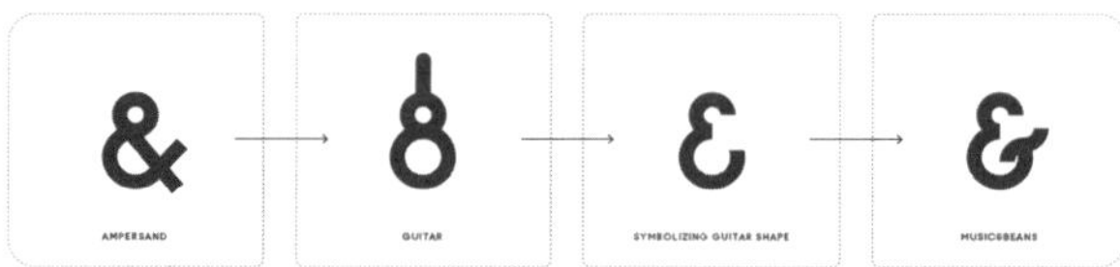

<u>The Objective</u>

After drinking your coffee and having your breakfast with freshly baked sourdough bread at Music & Beans, you can play any instrument you want in special soundproof rooms and even buy your favorite one!

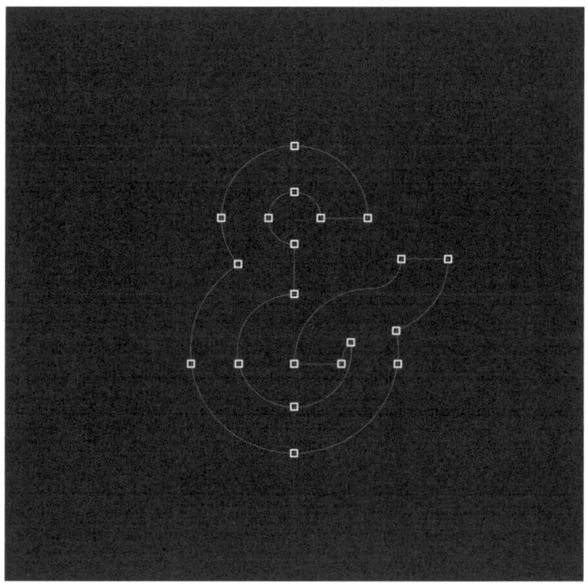

<u>The Solution</u>

We wanted to make an original work for this original shop. By blending the & symbol in the name with the guitar icon, we made a design that symbolizes the guitar and designed a new icon for the name. We mainly used black and white colors in our design. In addition to these colors, we used vertical lines in the design of products such as paper cups and aprons. These designs reminded us of the keys of a piano and allowed us to harmonize the branding with the theme. Thus, we achieved a modern and lively look with two classic colors. In addition, we preferred to follow a more colorful way in our poster design. We hope you like it too!

MUSIC&BEANS

MUSIC&BEANS

GIGAPPY PRESENTS LIVE MUSIC
FRIDAY 1ST FEBRUARY 2019
JOE
TAYLOR
CLOUDY
GALVEZ
RACHAEL
TRAVERS
gigappy
JAMESON
MUSIC&BEANS
CAMDEN

BERRY BLAST
4.6
ANTIOXIDANT SMOOTHIES
4.6
GREEEN SMOOTHIES
4.6
SUNSHINE
4.6
4.6

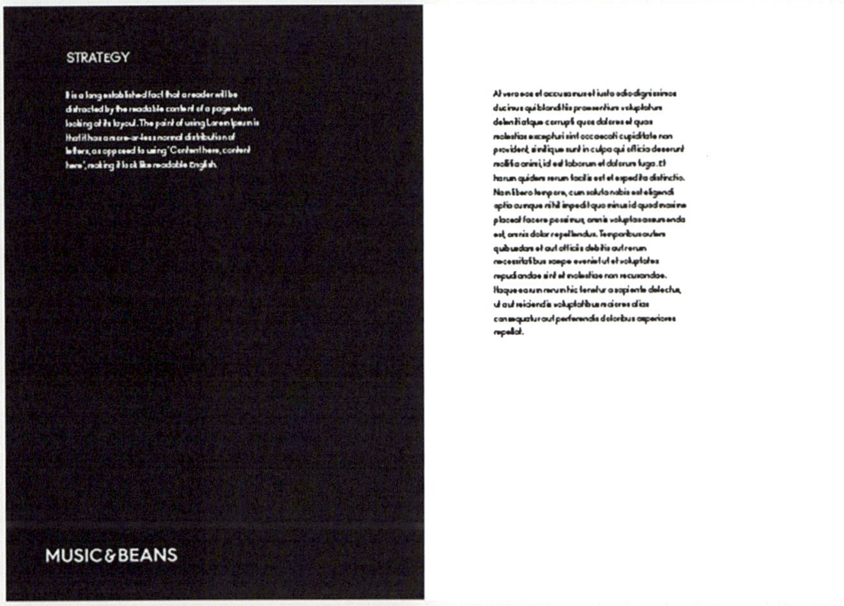
STRATEGY
It is a long established fact that a reader will be distracted by the readable content of a page when looking at its layout. The point of using Lorem Ipsum is that it has a more-or-less normal distribution of letters, as opposed to using 'Content here, content here', making it look like readable English.
MUSIC&BEANS
At vero eos et accusamus et iusto odio dignissimos ducimus qui blanditiis praesentium voluptatum deleniti atque corrupti quos dolores et quas molestias excepturi sint occaecati cupiditate non provident, similique sunt in culpa qui officia deserunt mollitia animi, id est laborum et dolorum fuga. Et harum quidem rerum facilis est et expedita distinctio. Nam libero tempore, cum soluta nobis est eligendi optio cumque nihil impedit quo minus id quod maxime placeat facere possimus, omnis voluptas assumenda est, omnis dolor repellendus. Temporibus autem quibusdam et aut officiis debitis aut rerum necessitatibus saepe eveniet ut et voluptates repudiandae sint et molestiae non recusandae. Itaque earum rerum hic tenetur a sapiente delectus, ut aut reiciendis voluptatibus maiores alias consequatur aut perferendis doloribus asperiores repellat.

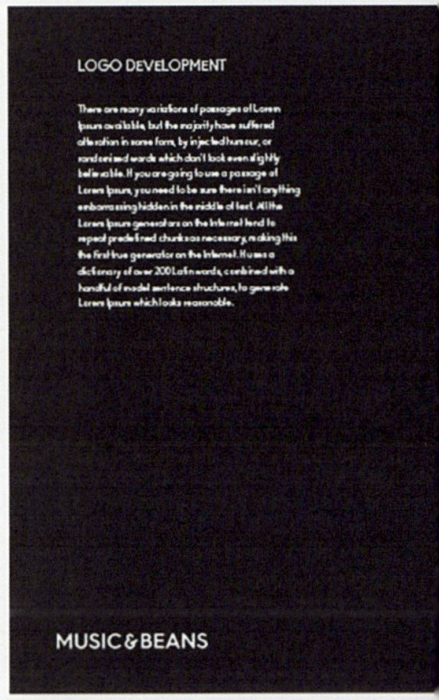
LOGO DEVELOPMENT
There are many variations of passages of Lorem Ipsum available, but the majority have suffered alteration in some form, by injected humour, or randomised words which don't look even slightly believable. If you are going to use a passage of Lorem Ipsum, you need to be sure there isn't anything embarrassing hidden in the middle of text. All the Lorem Ipsum generators on the Internet tend to repeat predefined chunks as necessary, making this the first true generator on the Internet. It uses a dictionary of over 200 Latin words, combined with a handful of model sentence structures, to generate Lorem Ipsum which looks reasonable.
MUSIC&BEANS

TONE
MUSIC&BEANS

BRANDING ELEMENTS
The standard chunk of Lorem Ipsum used since the 1500s is reproduced below for those interested. Sections 1.10.32 and 1.10.33 from "de Finibus Bonorum et Malorum" by Cicero are also reproduced in their exact original form, accompanied by English versions from the 1914 translation by H. Rackham.
MUSIC&BEANS

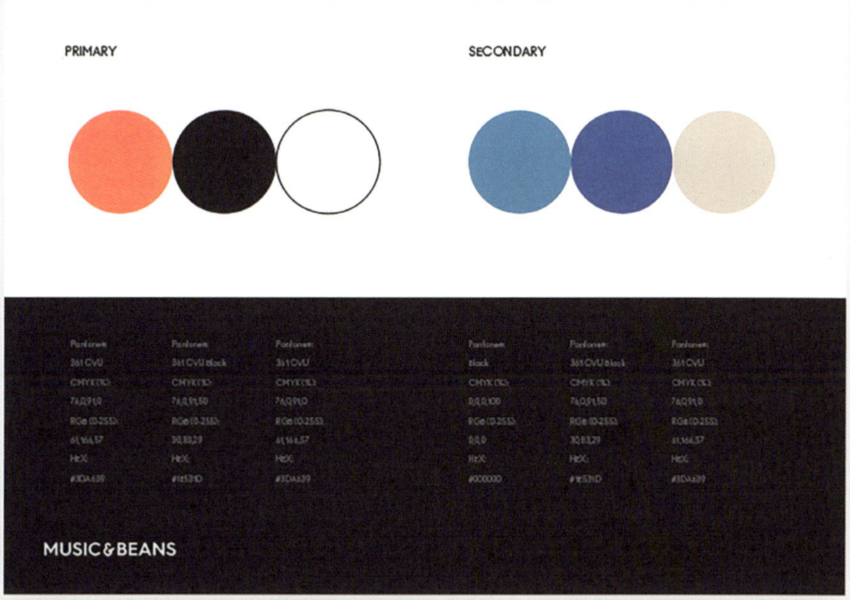
PRIMARY
SECONDARY
MUSIC&BEANS

MUSIC&BEANS

TONE
MUSIC&BEANS
MUSIC&BEANS

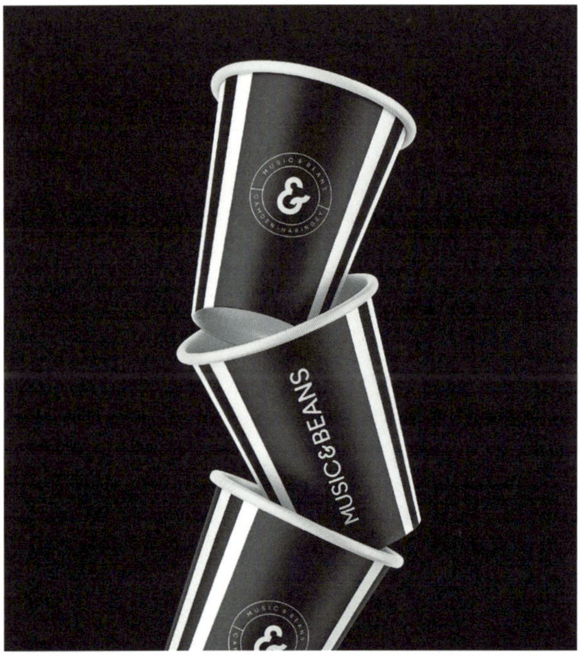
MUSIC&BEANS

MUSIC&BEANS

MUSIC
BEANS

MUSIC&BEANS

MUSIC&BEANS

MUSIC&BEANS

Designed by ***Uido Design Studio***

Orea coffee brewer

Physical product design and graphic design made by Uido Design Studio in 2020 - 2021

The world's most compact full-size coffee brewer. Orea reached out to Uido looking for a team to help him out in his venture of designing a brewer like none other. It had to be small, durable, aesthetic, had no screws, no moving parts, no assembly and to improve air flow over other brewers.

THE PROCESS
The design stage took several months in which we designed countless alternatives with different shapes, thickness and drainage patterns and sizes looking to perform the perfect speed of pouring. We tested the alternatives through functional prototypes till we achieved the desired result.

THE SOLUTION
We landed with something that delivers fast flow in a flat bed brewer - which helps extract brighter notes from coffee. Our approach solves a lot of the common problems around air flow, both inside the brewer and around it on the "feet". The Orea brewer is designed to optimise air flow - inside and outside the brewer. A lot of brewer designs lead to choking because air has a hard time going through and out and around the brewer.

The design removes everything that seemed unnecessary in coffee brewers in order to reduce size, weight, and to improve packability and compatibility.

Every brewer starts as a solid block of aluminium. It's then slowly carved out by sophisticated mills, leaving behind a beautiful and structurally strong unibody construction.
This helps with end-of-life recycling too - one solid aluminium item is a lot easier to recycle than an assembled multi-material product.

Orea is designed to fit in many existing outdoors camping cook systems and many common cups. We designed for versatility but didn't want it to feel like "an outdoorsy product" so that it can fit in the kitchen day to day too, It was not easy to strike that balance.

The brewer comes with a hand-finished optional-to-use leather sleeve. The sleeve helps with handling it when hot and helps improve heat retention while brewing - especially outdoors in variable temperatures.

Product name : OREA V2
Designed in collaboration with Orea.
Designer : Lautaro Lucero
Design studio : Uido Design Studio LLC

OREA

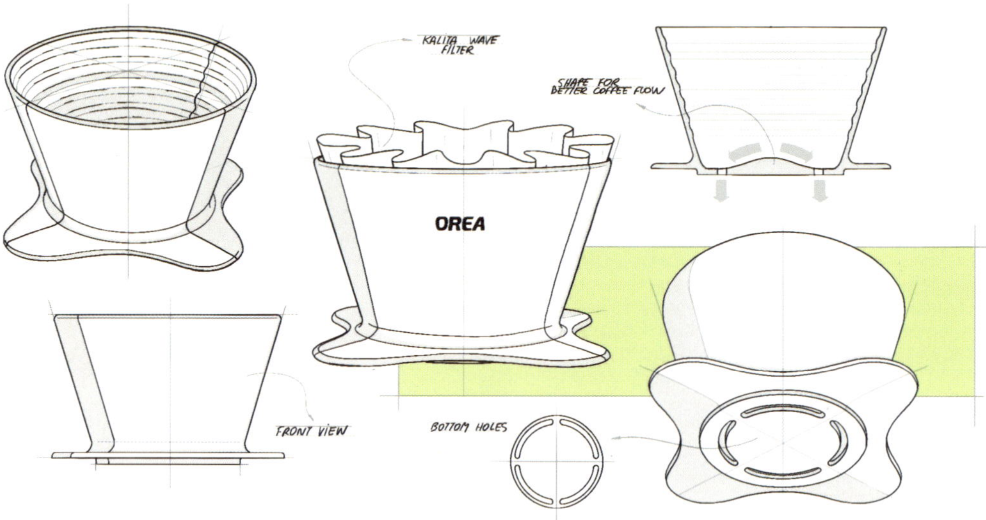
KALITA WAVE FILTER
SHAPE FOR BETTER COFFEE FLOW
OREA
FRONT VIEW
BOTTOM HOLES

OREA

OREA

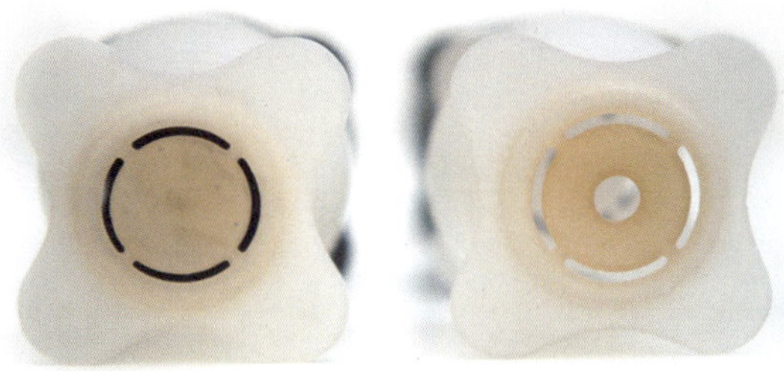

COFFEE
TAKESI
GEISHA
Produceret i
samarbejde med
Familien Iturralde
Ristedato:
28.12.20
Bedst Før:
28.03.21

OREA

OREA

Designed by **Monga Design**

PCB Seoul

Pray Coffe Bar (PCB) is a visual identity project created by designers from Florianópolis (Brazil) for a cafe and bar in Seoul, the South Korean capital. The client came to us when he saw that the studio's style matched the references he had for the project: jazz. The entire ambiance of the place refers to jazz bands, especially from the 40s to the 70s. The Altec A5 loudspeaker, used in theaters in the 60s, the Macintosh 240 radio valve, and many old records and other equipment from the period ... The name Pray Coffe Bar was inspired by the feelings that these songs evoke.

To represent the brand and all this atmosphere visually, we created an aesthetic that refers to old jazz record covers, through the typographic choices, colors and textures. The graphics present in the visual identity were inspired by some of the main instruments used in this musical style, such as the bass and piano.

The whole concept of naming, ambiance and visual identity was created remembering a time that doesn't seem so far away, when some people needed to "pray" for values such as freedom and human rights. It was necessary to sublimate anger, depression and desolation into Jazz.

프레이커피바
Pray Coffee Bar
Cigarretes
THERE ARE NO COMPETITORS, WE ALL ENJOY IT TOGETHER
PRAY COFFEE BAR SEOUL
기도 커피 바

프레이커피바
Pray Coffee Bar

프레이커피바
Pray
Coffee
Bar
프레이커피바
Pray
Coffee
Bar

프레이커피바
Pray
Coffee
Bar
기도 커피바
Pray
Coffee
Bar

Cigarretes
Love &
Pray Coffee Bar
THERE ARE NO COMPETITORS, WE ALL ENJOY IT TOGETHER
프레이
PRAY FOR THESE VALUES
커피바

프레이커피바
See you space cowboy...
DESIGNED BY @MONGADESIGN
PCB
Seoul
피씨비서울
FIND A SWEETNESS INSIDE BITTERNESS OF ESPRESSO.
우리를 따르라 @PCB_SEOUL

PCB
Seoul
Cigarretes
Love &

Designed by **kongsi design**

peep coffee

Peep coffee is a specialty coffee bar located at Bangsar, Kuala Lumpur — a neighbourhood area in an urban city. Half-hidden in a corner of @vernakular timepieces store, peep coffee bar creates a perfect moment to pause from the busy Bangsar. Peep's brand identity is designed with positive and cheerful vibes, because that's what we believe peep coffee is: energising. At Peep, everyone is passionate about sharing good moments & good coffee. From the name to the brand identity, we translate the concept to every corner, greeting everyone a good day ahead :) Peep this out @peepcoffee Good coffee is worth sharing, every moment is worth celebrating.

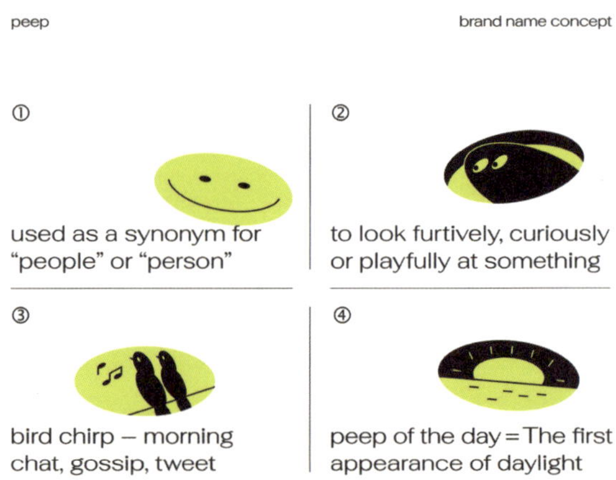

① **enhance the level of detail by adding ink trap**
② negative space inspired by coffee beans
③ expression, look around curiously and playfully
④ oval shape + 30° angle in different directions

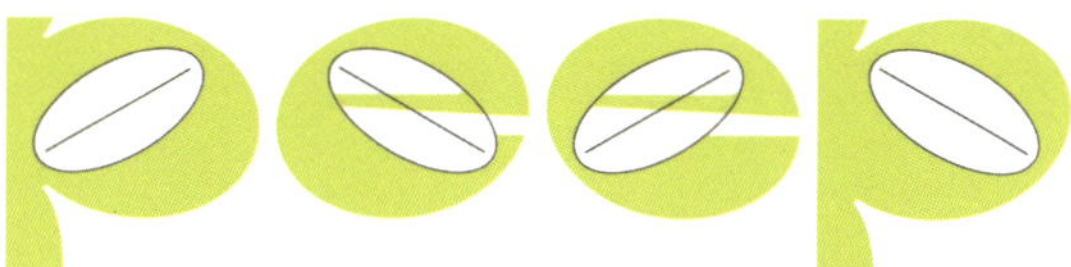

① enhance the level of detail by adding ink trap
② **negative space inspired by coffee beans**
③ expression, look around curiously and playfully
④ oval shape + 30° angle in different directions

① enhance the level of detail by adding ink trap
② negative space inspired by coffee beans
③ **expression, look around curiously and playfully**
④ oval shape + 30° angle in different directions

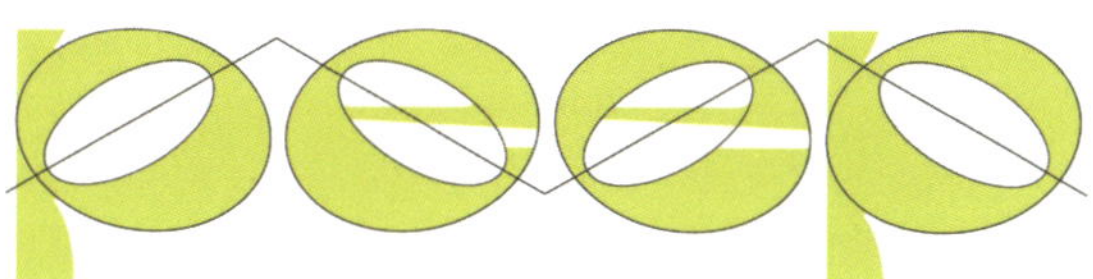

① enhance the level of detail by adding ink trap
② negative space inspired by coffee beans
③ expression, look around curiously and playfully
④ **oval shape + 30° angle in different directions**

peep

let's have coffee
peep coffee — A specialty coffee shop located at Bangsar, Kuala Lumpur, MY — a neighbourhood area in an urban city. We believe good coffee is worth sharing, every moment is worth celebrating

peep

peep

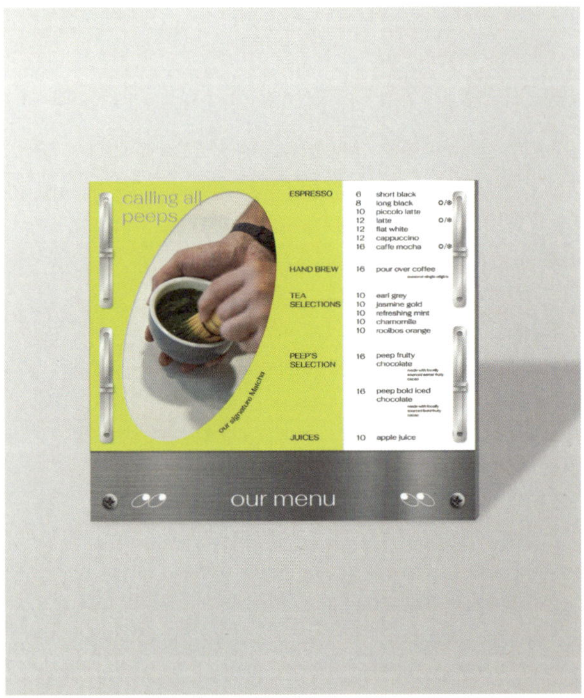
calling all peeps
our signature Matcha
ESPRESSO
6 short black
8 long black
10 piccolo latte
12 latte
12 flat white
12 cappuccino
16 caffe mocha
HAND BREW
16 pour over coffee
TEA SELECTIONS
10 earl grey
10 jasmine gold
10 refreshing mint
10 chamomile
10 rooibos orange
PEEP'S SELECTION
16 peep fruity chocolate
16 peep bold iced chocolate
JUICES
10 apple juice
our menu

peep
peep

ETHIOPIA YIRGACHEFFE G1
HONEY HAFURSA WARO

peep
peep this out
peep

get 1 cup free
with 10 purchase
*T&C APPLY
for more updates, visit our ig @peepcoffee

peep
with 10 purchase
for more updates, visit our ig @peepcoffee

peep

bye peeps
bye peeps

coffee?
open daily 7:30am-10pm
peep

peep

pick up here

peep
peep

am-10pm

peep this out
peep this out
peep
vernakular
coffee?
open daily 7:30am-10pm
peep

peep

peep of the day

peep

peep

ESPRESSO
6 short black
8 long black
10 piccolo latte
12 latte
12 flat white
12 cappuccino
16 caffe mocha
HAND BREW
20 pour over coffee
TEA SELECTIONS
10 earl grey
10 jasmine gold
10 refreshing mint
10 chamomile
10 rooibos orange
PEEP'S SELECTION
16 peep fruity chocolate
16 peep bold iced chocolate
JUICES
10 apple juice
our menu

peep

coffee?
open daily 7:30am-10pm
peep
peep

Designed by ***Studio leM***

Plouf

Plouf Coffee, located in Yeonnam-dong, Seoul, sells drinks such as wine, coffee, and beverages, and bakeries such as scones, meringue, and cakes under the concept of a British bakery cafe. For this project, we designed the overall visual and applications using the brand emblem developed by Catherine Potvin's character illustration and Simon Langlois's logotype. The combination of the drawing touch of the main character and the witty San Serif logotype is used as a signature element. Moreover, we set blue and ivory as the main colors and pink and orange-red as sub-colors which are applied to the components of the application.

Plouf
Plouf
coffee/Bakery/Wine

plouf
plouf
plouf
plouf
plouf
plouf

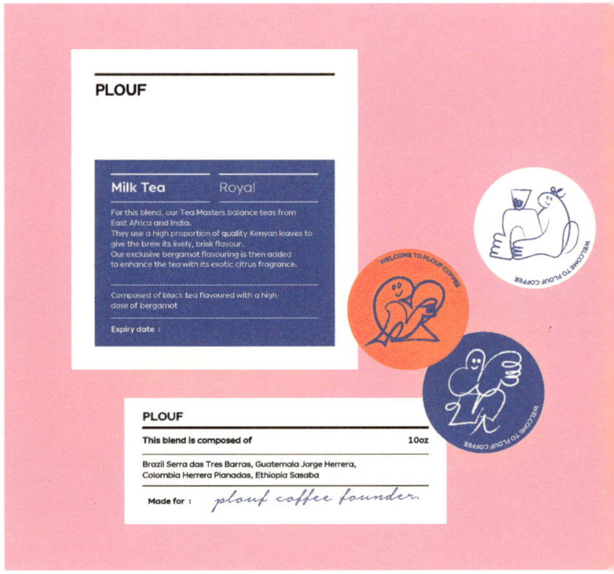
PLOUF
Milk Tea
Royal
For this blend, our Tea Masters balance teas from East Africa and India.
They use a high proportion of quality Kenyan leaves to give the brew its lively, brisk flavour.
Our exclusive bergamot flavouring is then added to enhance the tea with its exotic citrus fragrance.
Composed of black tea flavoured with a high dose of bergamot
Expiry date :
WELCOME TO PLOUF COFFEE
PLOUF
This blend is composed of
10oz
Brazil Serra das Tres Barras, Guatemala Jorge Herrera, Colombia Herrera Planadas, Ethiopia Sasaba
Made for :
plouf coffee founder.

NON - COFFEE
Fruit Punch

NOTIC
DESSERT
It is recommended to eat within 2 days of purchase, and it can be stored in the freezer until 30 days.

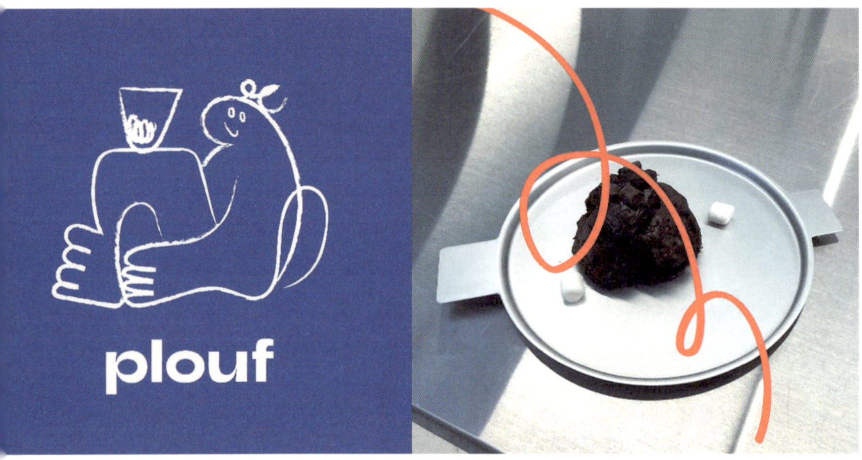
plouf

Latte / Ade / Tea /Juice
Chocolate Latte
Strawberry Latte
Lemon Ade
Grapefruit Ade
Fruit Punch
Tea
Chamomile
Green Tea
Earl Grey
Peppermint

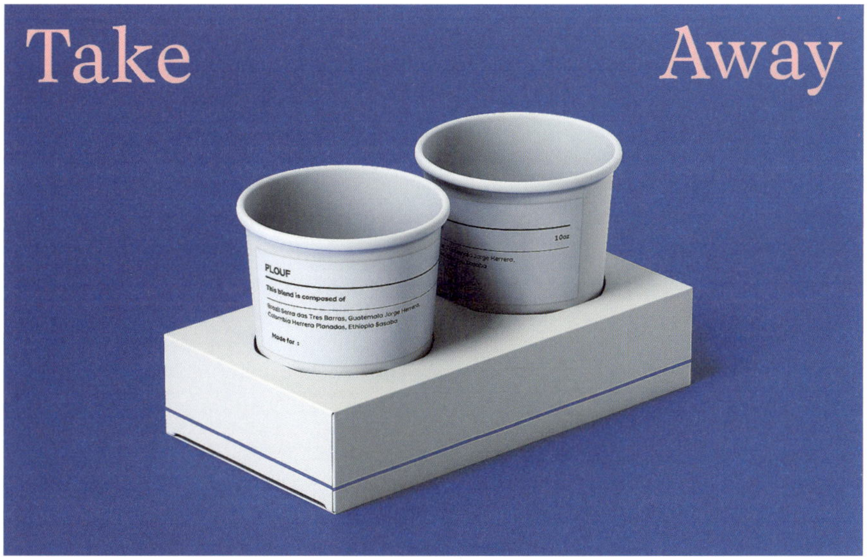
Take
Away
PLOUF
This blend is composed of
Made for :

12, Donggyo-ro 46-gil,
Mapo-gu, Seoul, Republic of Korea
Plouf
Coffee /
plouf
Coffee / Bakery / Wine

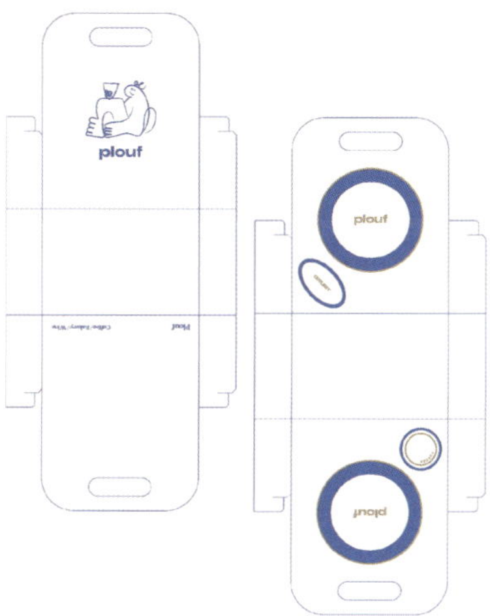
plouf

plouf

plouf

Plouf
Plouf
coffee/Bakery/Wine
Plouf
Plouf
coffee/Bakery/Wine
Plouf
Plouf
coffee/Bakery/Wine

Plouf
Plouf
[Cake]
[Chocolate Cake]
Plouf
Plouf
[Scone]
[Wine]

Plouf coffee/Bakery/Wine
EARL GREY SCONE 4.3

Designed by **Studio Woork**

PROJECT Sangrai 1.0

PROJECT Sangrai is a project initiated by Kopikalyan where people, especially coffee enthusiasts can collaborate and inspire each other whilst promoting coffees of Indonesia to a bigger market, in their own way.

Kopikalyan Roastery showcases Indonesian coffees that are curated specially according to their own different and unique theme, from each collection. Every month, a figure of Indonesian coffee expert like Muhammad Aga, Muhammad Fakhri, Ryan Wibawa, etc will be invited to Kopikalyan Roastery, and create from two types of high quality Indonesian coffees to be served and enjoyed.

www.kopikalyan.com

<u>*Additional:*</u>

The logo identity design for PROJECT Sangrai 1.0 is inspired by the rotating movement of a coffee roasting machine. The packaging for PROJECT Sangrai 1.0 comes in the shape of a box with an easy pulling access that holds two bags of Kopikalyan high quality ground coffee beans. We use a pop of blue color for the branding concept of PROJECT Sangrai 1.0, to respond the muted earth tones of Kopikalyan's cafe environment. Creating a fresh look that seek attention at the same time.

Design team: Io Woo, Danang Abiyoso
Client: Kopi Kalyan
Location (complete address): 19, Barito II, South Jakarta, Indonesia
Photographer: Studio Woork

PROJECT
PROJECT Sangrai
Sangrai 1.0
1.0

PROJECT

PROJECT
SANGRAI
1.0
PROJECT
Sangrai
1.0
SOSOK KALYAN
Bitter

PROJECT
SANGRAI
1.0
PROJECT
Sangrai
1.0
SOSOK KALYAN
Bitter

Sangrai 1.0 • PRO
Good
Coffee

PROJECT
Sangrai
1.0
SOSOK KALYAN
Bitter

PROJECT Sangrai 1.0
PROCESS
REGION
250G
TASTING NOTES
VARIETY
MASL
KOPIKALYAN ROASTERY

PROJECT Sangrai 1.0
PROCESS
REGION
250G
TASTING NOTES
VARIETY
MASL
KOPIKALYAN ROASTERY
PROJECT Sangrai 1.0
PROJECT Sangrai 1.0

1.0
PROJECT
Sangrai

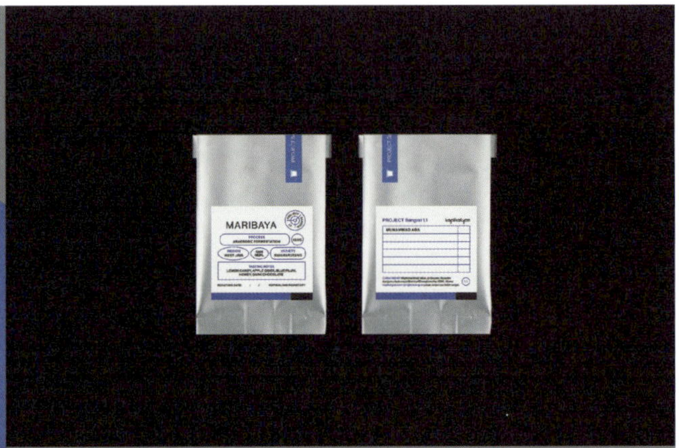
MARIBAYA

1.0

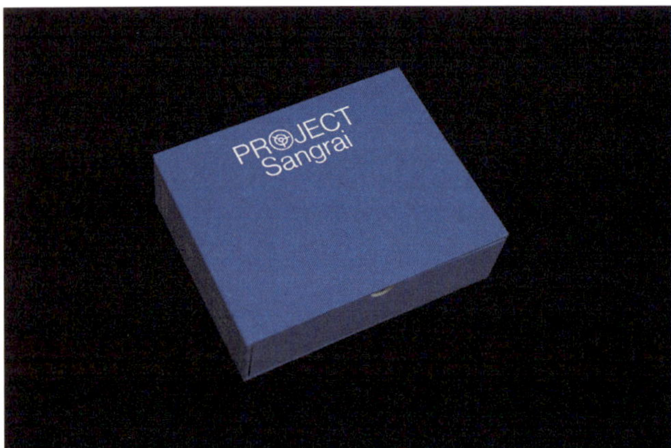
PROJECT
Sangrai

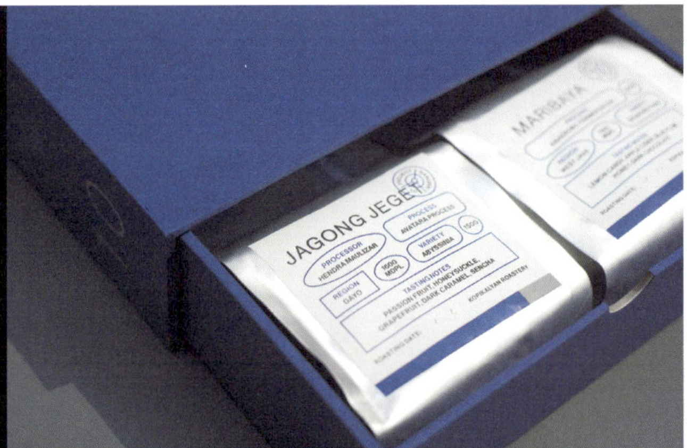
MARIBAYA

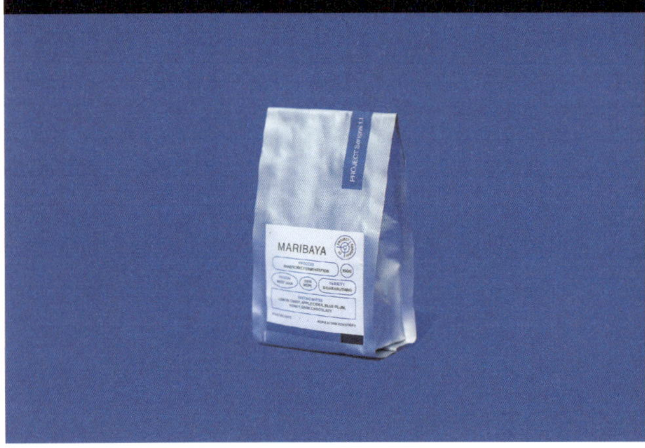
MARIBAYA

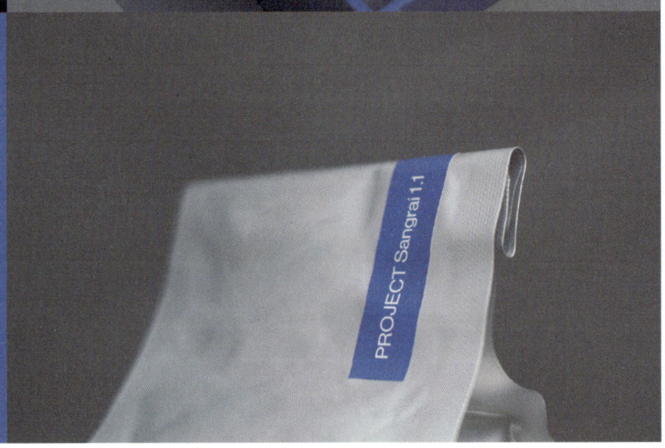
PROJECT Sangrai 1.1

PROJECT
Sangrai

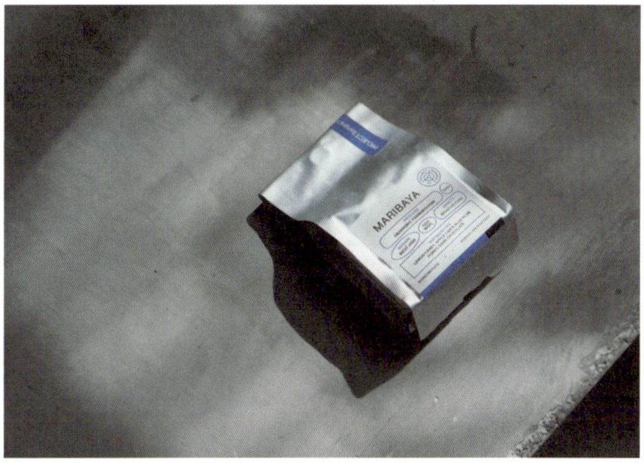
MARIBAYA

KOPIKALYAN
ROASTERY
1.0

MARIBAYA

PROJECT
Sangrai

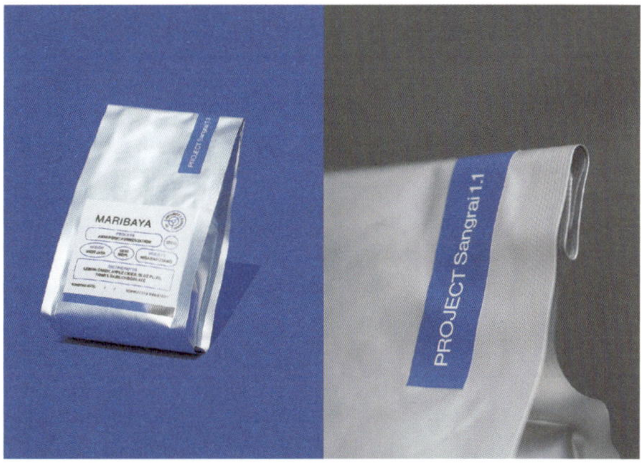
MARIBAYA
PROJECT Sangrai 1.1

KOPIKALYAN
ROASTERY

PROJECT
Sangrai
KOPIKALYAN
ROASTERY
1.0

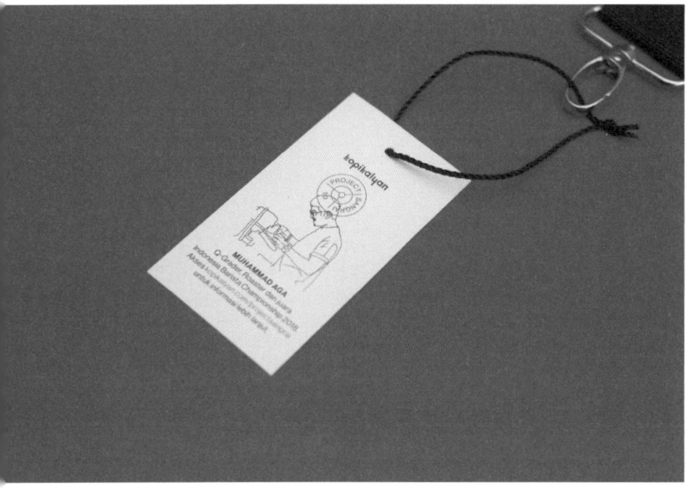
kopikalyan
MUHAMMAD AGA

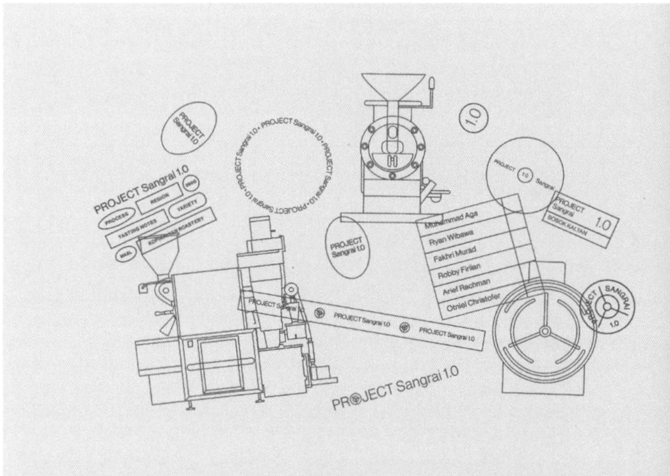
PROJECT Sangrai 1.0
PROJECT Sangrai 1.0
Muhammad Aga
Ryan Wibawa
Fakhri Murad
Robby Firlian
Arief Rachman
Otniel Christofer
1.0
PROJECT Sangrai 1.0

PROJECT
Sangrai 1.1
X
Muhammad
Aga
KEYCHAIN

Bitter
Sweet
Coffee
Please
PROJECT SANGRAI 1.0
1.0 · PROJECT Sangrai 1.0 · PROJECT
PROJECT Sangrai 1.0
1.0
PROJECT
Sangrai
1.0
SOSOK KALYAN

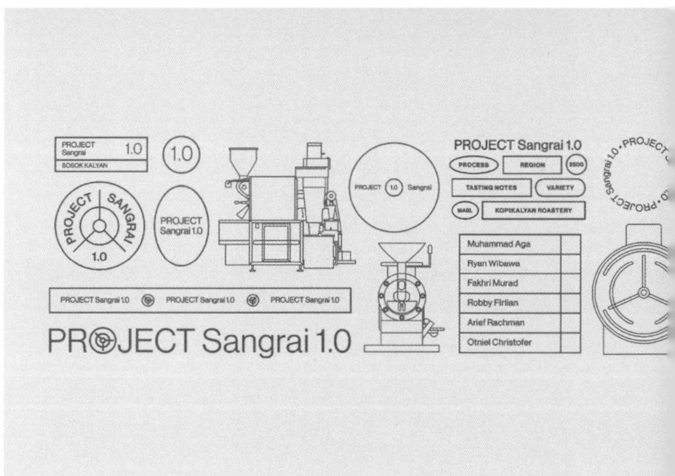
PROJECT
Sangrai
1.0
SOSOK KALYAN
1.0
PROJECT SANGRAI 1.0
PROJECT Sangrai 1.0
PROJECT 1.0 Sangrai
PROJECT Sangrai 1.0
PROCESS
REGION
TASTING NOTES
VARIETY
KOPIKALYAN ROASTERY
Muhammad Aga
Ryan Wibawa
Fakhri Murad
Robby Firlian
Arief Rachman
Otniel Christofer
PROJECT Sangrai 1.0
PROJECT Sangrai 1.0
PROJECT Sangrai 1.0
PROJECT Sangrai 1.0

PROJECT Sangrai 1.0

PROJECT Sangrai 1.0
PROCESS
REGION
TASTING NOTES
VARIETY
KOPIKALYAN ROASTERY

PROJECT Sangrai 1.0
REGION
250G
PROCESS
VARIETY
TASTING NOTES
KOPIKALYAN ROASTERY
MASL

PROJECT
Sangrai 1.0
kopikalyan
Sebuah project untuk menjadikan ruang sangrai Kopikalyan wadah bagi orang-orang inspiratif berkolaborasi memperkenalkan kopi Indonesia ke pasar yang lebih luas dengan caranya masing-masing. Kopikalyan Roastery menampilkan kopi Indonesia yang spesial dikurasi dengan mengikuti tema yang berbeda di setiap koleksinya.
Project Sangrai 1.0 berjudul SOSOK KALYAN. Setiap bulannya, satu figur perkopian Indonesia akan mampir ke ruang sangrai Kopikalyan, mengkurasi dua kopi berkualitas Indonesia untuk bisa dinikmati kalyan selama sebulan penuh.
PROJECT
PROJECT Sangrai
Sangrai 1.0
1.0

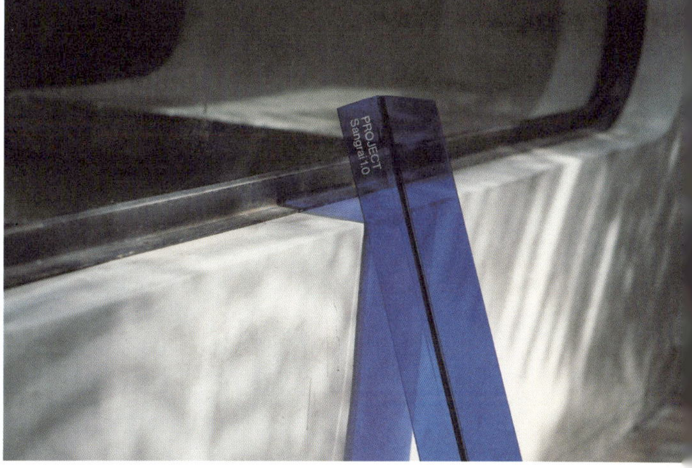
PROJECT
Sangrai 1.0

PROJECT
Sangrai 1.0

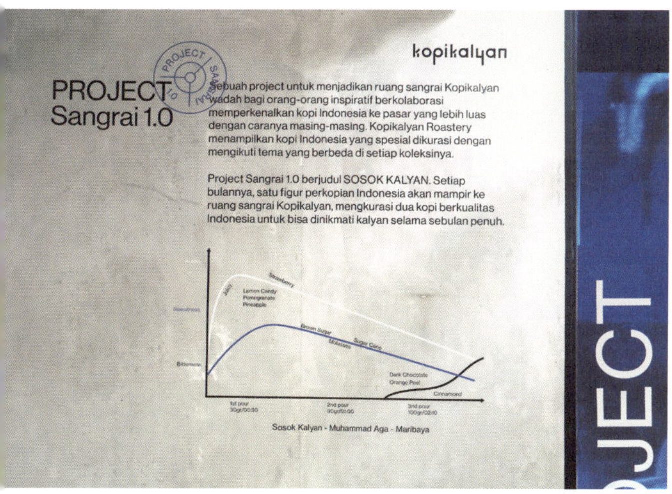
kopikalyan
PROJECT
Sangrai 1.0
Sebuah project untuk menjadikan ruang sangrai Kopikalyan wadah bagi orang-orang inspiratif berkolaborasi memperkenalkan kopi Indonesia ke pasar yang lebih luas dengan caranya masing-masing. Kopikalyan Roastery menampilkan kopi Indonesia yang spesial dikurasi dengan mengikuti tema yang berbeda di setiap koleksinya.
Project Sangrai 1.0 berjudul SOSOK KALYAN. Setiap bulannya, satu figur perkopian Indonesia akan mampir ke ruang sangrai Kopikalyan, mengkurasi dua kopi berkualitas Indonesia untuk bisa dinikmati kalyan selama sebulan penuh.
Sosok Kalyan - Muhammad Aga - Maribaya
JECT

PROJECT
SANGRAI
1.0

Designed by ***Sabhat KK Rak***

RAWR Café

RAWR is about the contrast between the elegance of coffee and the power of caffeine. The main mission of RAWR is to portray the nature of drinking coffee into one simple logo.

The team started out by clarifying the basics of what the cafe is. RAWR is a cafe that specializes in coffee, located at Naiipa (meaning in the forest) Private Office Space, Bangkok, Thailand. The cafe itself is surrounded by trees which have stood resolutely for over thirty years. Therefore it is a place where people can escape from the high-rises, pollution, chaos of city life and enjoy a nice cup of coffee. The name RAWR signifies where coffee and forest intersects.

The beauty of coffee is its character. Visually; when you see a cup or someone drinking coffee, you get the sense of something simple, smart and elegant. On the other hand caffeine gives you power and energy. To visualize something that is so simple and stable yet powerful and energetic at the same time is the challenge of this project.

The grid of the logo comes from the shape that symbolizes the three key elements of the cafe - the coffee bean, coffee tube and the name "RAWR" itself.

RAWR
CAFÉ
OPENING HOURS
WEEKENDS
9AM – 8PM
10AM – 7PM
CLOSED ON THURSDAYS

RAWR
RAWR CAF
RAWR

RAWR
CAFÉ

RAWR

RAWR
TALK LESS
RAWR MORE
BOLD TO BE

RAWR

RAWR
TALK LESS
RAWR MORE

RAWR
RAWR
RAWR

RAWR

RAWR

RAWR

RAWR

RAWR
CAFÉ

RAWR
CAFÉ

CREM

RAWR

Designed by **low key Design**

SLAB TOWN COFFEE

Concept:「We collected the fragments and gradually polished them into a" complete "slab.」

At the beginning of the year, we received the commission from Seven, the manager of SLAB TOWN, to design the vision for his new brand. After listening to Seven's general ideas and concepts, we were more in favor and appreciate it As expected, we made very smooth progress.

The LOGO was basically confirmed in the first week of the proposal, and there was enough time left to sample the materials. Thanks to Seven, the plane vision of SLAB TOWN COFFEE, which we cooperated with, could be presented.

"The idea comes from a hippie town in a movie into the wild, which really exists in the desert of Southern California. Originally named slab city. I prefer the word town, so I changed it. "-Seven

When we tried to understand the real Slab City, which is completely free without government restrictions, we are shocked that it has no water and no electricity. In the hottest summer, the temperature can reach 50 degrees. So many free souls live in this city in which the condition is unfriendly to live. Every household has a power generation plate on the room or car roof. This power generation plate is a "slab" of a sudden flash of light for us, and SLAB itself means "a slab" So we try to draw a "slab" from different perspectives, which seems to be a very simple geometric figure.

We constantly adjust the scale to make it appear the most comfortable way in our minds. Typesetting the English LOGO on the slate seems to be just right, with a little retro feeling, which is just what we want.

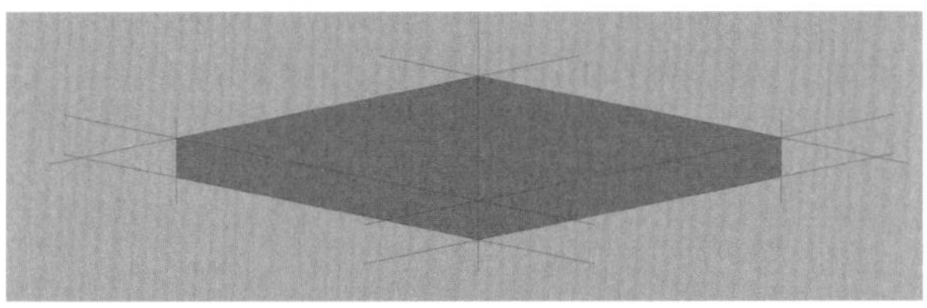

SLAB TOWN
SLAB TOWN
SLAB TOWN
SLAB TOWN

SLAB TOWN

SLAB TOWN
COFFEE
SLAB TOWN
COFFEE
SLAB TOWN
COFFEE
SLAB TOWN
COFFEE
Espresso
Pour Over
Others
COFFEE
SLAB TOWN
Happiness only real when shared.

COFFEE
SLAB TOWN
Dark Roasted
Brazil San Paulo - Pulped Natural 60%
Ethiopia Yirgacheffe - Natural 40%
Flavor Notes
Tobacco \ Cranberry \ Dark Chocolate
Slab Town Blend
COFFEE
SLAB TOWN
Light Roasted
Region: Samaipata, Santa Cruz
Altitude: 1600m- 1650m | Process: Washed
Farm: Finca Tacu
Variety: Java
Flavor Notes
Lemon-tea like \ Very Sweet
Bolivia
COFFEE
SLAB TOWN
Light Roasted
PNG Baroida -Washed 50%
Costa Rica Canet Raisin -Honey 30%
Ethiopia Chelelektu -Natural 10%
Ethiopia Worka -Washed 10%
Flavor Notes
Orange \ Cranberry \ Peach
Olive Blend
COFFEE
SLAB TOWN
Light Roasted
Region: Renacimiento, Chiriqui
Altitude: 1400m-1700m | Process: Natural, Sun-Dried
Farm: Saint Claire
Variety: Central America Gesha
Flavor Notes
Orange \ Peach \ Honeyed-like sweet
Panama
COFFEE
SLAB TOWN
Light Roasted
Region: Gedeb,Gedeo,SNNPR
Altitude: 1950m-2100m | Process: Washed
Farm: Worka Sakaro
Variety: Heirloom (Kumie, Diga, Wilsho)
Flavor Notes
Orange \ Floral \ Earl Grey Tea-like
Ethiopia
COFFEE
SLAB TOWN
Light Roasted
Region: Ajuya Valley
Altitude: 1800m-1865m | Process: Washed
Farm: Colbran
Variety: Arusha / K7
Flavor Notes
Orange \ Cherry \ Cane Sugar Sweet
PNG

SLAB TOWN
COFFEE

SLAB TOWN

BONOX
SLAB TOWN
COFFEE
S-8oz L-12oz
18
18
22
Espresso
Espresso
Americano
Latte
Flat White

COFFEE
SLAB TOWN

SLAB TOWN
COFFEE
SLAB TOWN
COFFEE
SLAB TOWN
COFFEE

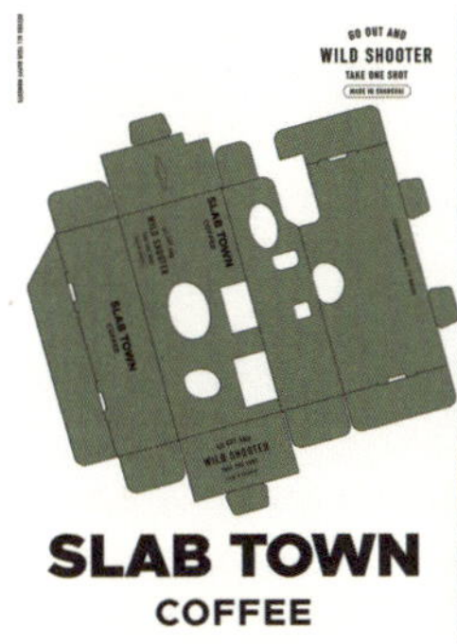
GO OUT AND
WILD SHOOTER
TAKE ONE SHOT
SLAB TOWN
COFFEE

LET'S 露营
CAMPING
GO OUT HUNTING #GO OUT HUNTING #GO OUT HUNTING

SLAB TOWN — Donghu Road — Fenyang Road — Middle Fuxing Road — East Fuxing Road Ferry — Dongchang Road Ferry — Pudong Binjiang Cycling Path — South Pier Ferry — Lujiangbang Ferry — Middle Longhua Road — Dong'an Road — Changle Road — SLAB TOWN
09.05 Sat.
RIDE
THE WILD
19:00-21:00
50 RMB / Person
Limited to 20 persons
SLAB TOWN tokyobike
SLAB TOWN tokyobike

NATURAL WINE
TASTING
Domaine JAMBON &
Une Tranche Paradis 2018
Dynamitage 2019
Sein pour Sein 2018
NELEMAN Viognier Verdil
NELEMAN Chardonnay Muscat
Marie Rose 2019
19:00-21:00
Nov.14th 2020
自然酒品鉴

SLAB TOWN — Donghu Road — Fenyang Road — Middle Fuxing Road — East Fuxing Road Ferry — Dongchang Road Ferry — Pudong Binjiang Cycling Path — South Pier Ferry — Lujiangbang Ferry — Middle Longhua Road — Dong'an Road — Changle Road — SLAB TOWN
09.05 Sat.
RIDE
THE WILD
19:00-21:00
50 RMB / Person
Limited to 20 persons
SLAB TOWN tokyobike
SLAB TOWN tokyobike

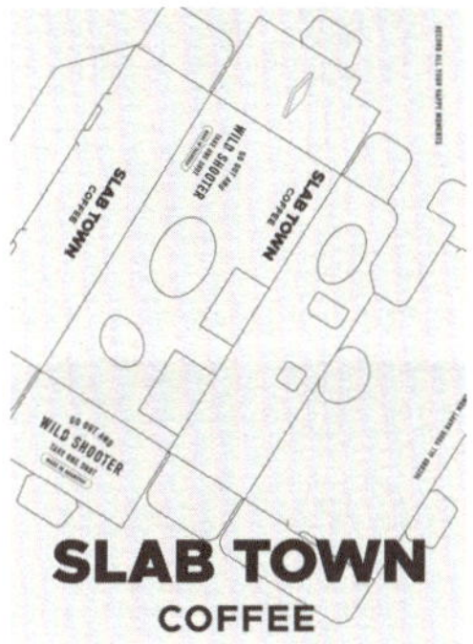
SLAB TOWN
COFFEE
WILD SHOOTER
SLAB TOWN
COFFEE

已
上线。
SLAB TOWN
COFFEE DELIVERY
HAS BEEN
LAUNCHED
NEWS
COFFEE DELIVERY
HAS BEEN
LAUNCHED
美团
外卖

10.14
Join us for free
Limited to 15 persons
5km
LET'S
RUN
Wed.
19:00-20:00
RUNNING

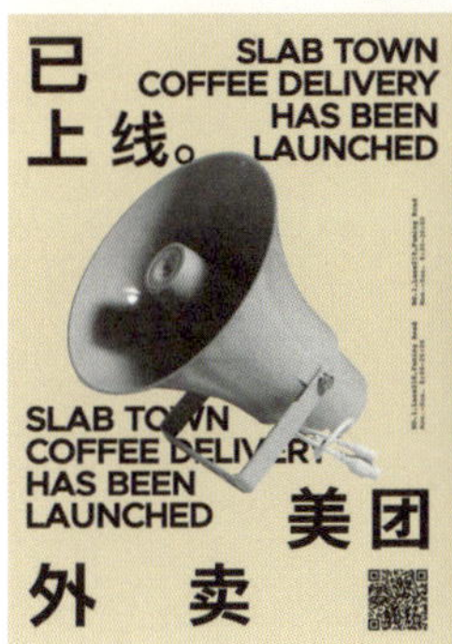
已
上线。
SLAB TOWN
COFFEE DELIVERY
HAS BEEN
LAUNCHED
美团
外卖

LET'S
Sat.
CUPPING
10:00-12:00
08.29
Papua New Guinea Washed / Yunnan Natural
Costa Rica Raisin Honey / Colombia Honey
Kenya Washed / Panama Natural / Costa Rica Washed
Ethiopia Washed / Colombia Washed / Ethiopia Natural

Designed by **Marka Works**

Spout

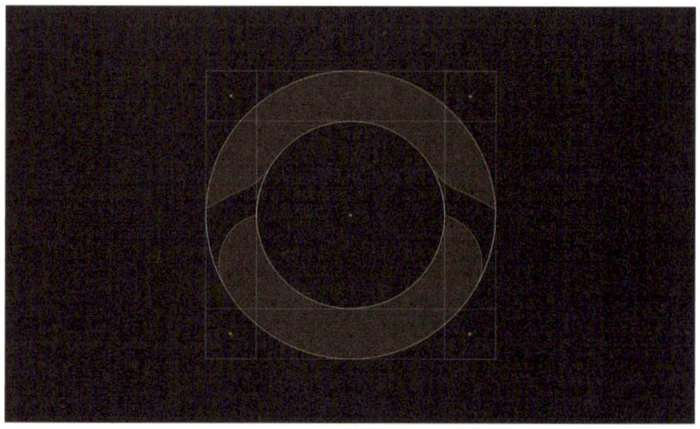

The Client

Spout is a coffee shop established in Saudi Arabia that offers high quality coffee to its customers.

The Objective

Spout offers daily, fresh desserts and fresh beverages with unique flavors as well as the perfectly roasted coffee as they use high quality coffee beans.

The Solution

When we were creating the brand identity of Spout, we wanted to emphasize the high quality coffee and the luxurious and bold look with gold and black color tones. We created a remarkable and powerful logo design by using the letter 'O' in its name. Besides, the main reason why we used the letter 'O' in the logo was to create a logo that complements the brand by almost uniting the upper part of the letter 'O' to the lower part as to resemble it to the coffee spoon in coffee machines. For the design of the menus, we aimed to give a simple, yet stylish look. We have also created poster designs that gives a bold impression, as well as the cool takeaway cups and boxes' designs.

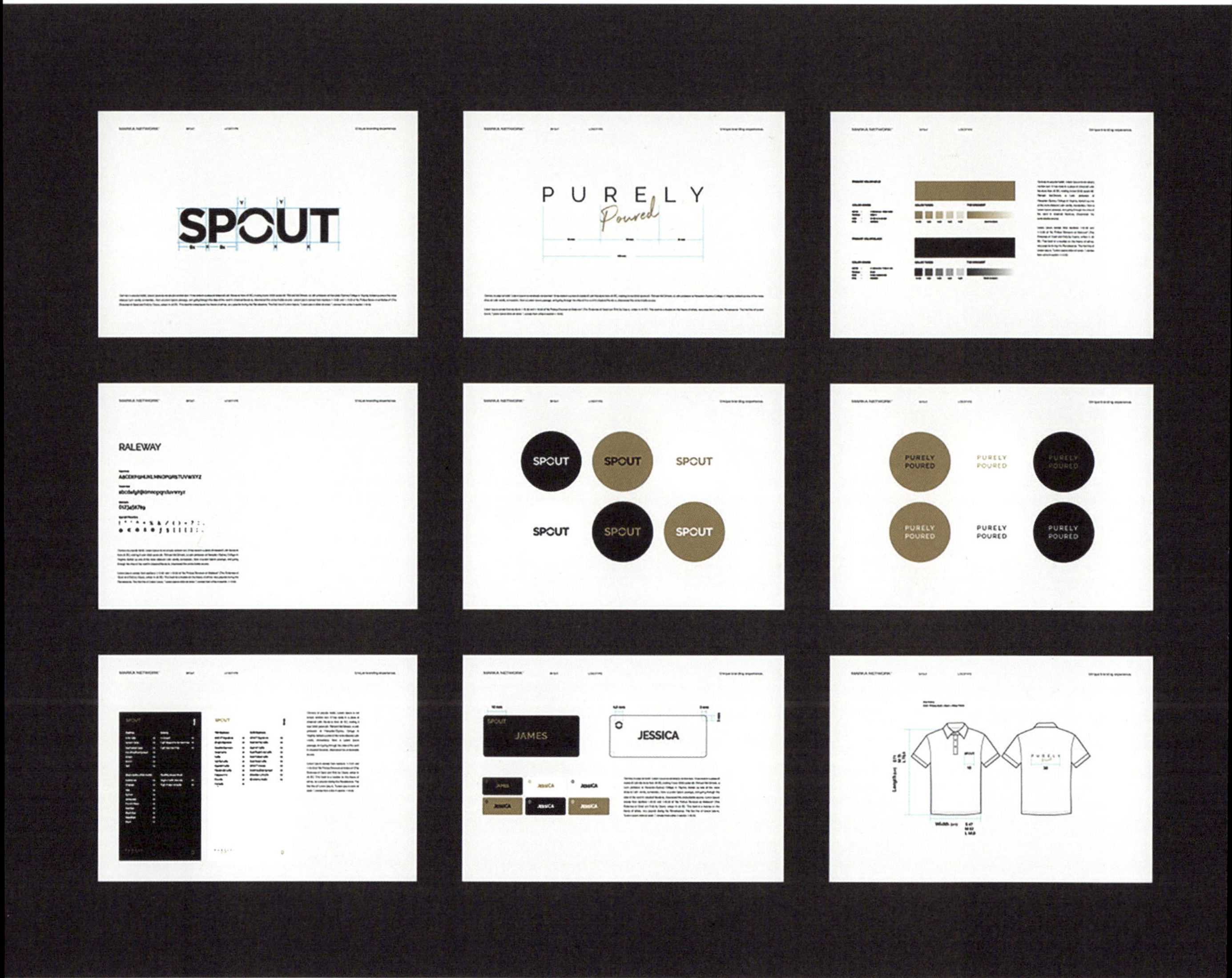
SPOUT
PURELY
Poured
RALEWAY
JAMES
JESSICA

PURELY
Poured
SPOUT

SPOUT
Foods
Pastries
Milk Cake
Lemon Cake
Red Velvet Cake
Marshmallow Spread
Eclear
Donut
Tart
Black Coffee (Hot/Cold)
Cold Brew
Chemex
V60
Siphon
Aeropress
French Press
Red Eye
Black Eye
Dead Eye
Black
Healthy Snack Food
Yoghurt with Granola
High Protein Snacks
SPOUT
Drinks
Hot Espresso
SPOUT Espresso
Single Espresso
Double Espresso
Americano
Latte
Vanilla Latte
Spanish Latte
Hazelnuts Latte
Cappuccino
Piccolo
Cortado
Cold Espresso
SPOUT Signature
Iced Vanilla Latte
Spanish Latte
Iced Hazelnuts Latte
Iced Flakes Latte
Iced Rose Latte
SPOUT Crema
Marshmallow Spread
Strawberry Mojito
Blueberry Mojito

HIGHEST QUALITY
IN EVERY CUP OF
COFFEE
INSTAGRAM.COM/SPOUT.SA
SPOUT
THE ZONE MALL
PURELY
NEW
IN
TOWN
THE ZONE MALL

PURELY
INSTAGRAM.COM/SPOUT.SA
NEW
IN
TOWN
THE ZONE MALL
SPECIALITY
COFFEE
INSTAGRAM.COM/SPOUT.SA
SPOUT
THE ZONE MALL

SPOUT
The Zone, Riyadh
PURELY
Specialty Coffee

SPOUT

SPOUT

SPOUT

SPOUT

PURELY

SPOUT

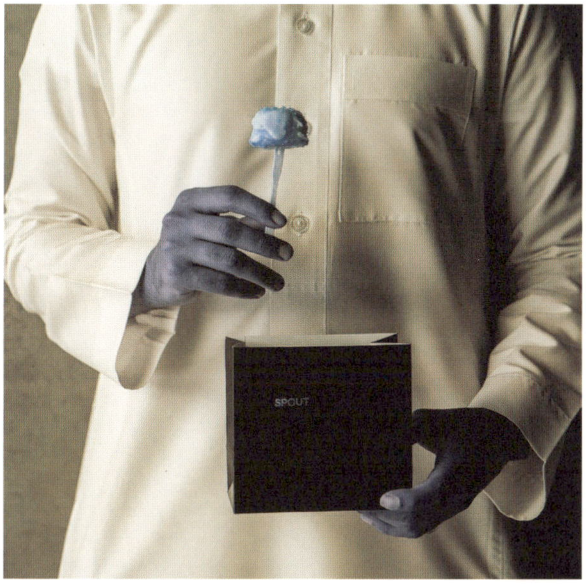
SPOUT

PURELY

Designed by **low key Design**

STAYTION

The name Staytion contains two English words: stay and station. Stay means to stay, staytion hope customers can find a reason to stay. Station: Station, staytion hope the guests can start again when they take a break in staytion. The brand pattern is an extension design from the letter "y". We apply this brand pattern to many material designs to provide brand integrity and high recognition.

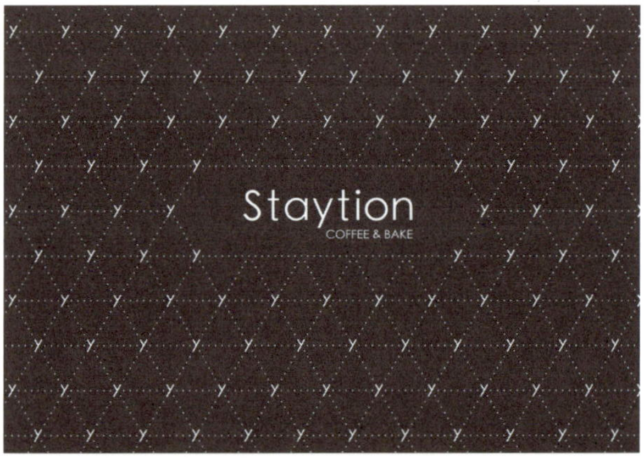

Together
80ml
whipping cream
espresso
baileys

Staytion
101
101吐司 TOAST 原味
Staytion

Staytion
COFFEE & BAKE
MENU
THE REASON
TO SATY

Staytion
COFFEE & BAKE

Staytion
COFFEE & BAKE

101
17

Designed by ***Uido Design Studio***

The Sense Cup

Coffee Tasting Cup

The Sense Cup is a specialty coffee cup designed to enhance perception of aromatics, brightness, and sweetness. The ceramic body is wine glass in form, with a narrow neck that promotes concentrated evaporation and higher intensity of aroma. The tulip style lip creates a wide surface area that introduces the beverage to the palate - enhancing perceptions of coffee's complex and delicate aromas.

With a capacity of 150ml, the Sense Cup is designed to pair with a carafe. Delightful to hold, extremely enjoyable to drink from, and optimized for the perfect sensory experience - enjoy coffee like never before.

THE PROCESS

We tested dozen of variations in the search of the perfect form. We not only wanted to design a cup that would look cute, but we also wanted to find a way to enhance the aroma, sweetness and brightness in the coffee.

Before starting industrial production, we made two plaster molds to test the cup, and also to test different color and texture finishes using different types of oxides and enamels. These were some of the first ceramic prototypes of Sense.

Designed in collaboration with Orea.
Designer : Lautaro Lucero

FINAL 1

Sense
Sense
coffee tasting cup
Enhanced aromatics and flavour in coffee.
150ml
White

Designed by **Marka Works**

The Supreme Roastering Co.

The Client

The Supreme Roastering Co., a coffee producer based in San Francisco, CA. We designed their brand identity in order to provide them with a vintage and minimal look.

The Objective

It is a design in which we wish to give us the real coffee experience with coffees in different aromas produced from the high quality coffee beans.

The Solution

For Supreme, we initially chose dark tones, but then decided to create a subtle contrast with the orange color. In addition, we used light and soft colors as complementary. During our brand identity formulation process, we integrated Supreme typography which has a more vintage look, with the typography in Roastering Co. which has a more minimal look. We have adopted a simple and easy-to-understand style in the label design. In addition to product designs such as takeaway cups and coasters, we created a unique design by using different combinations of the same colors and patterns on each packaging design. We hope you like it too!

The Supreme
ROASTERING CO.

The Supreme
ROASTERING CO.

STRATEGY
THE SUPREME ROASTERING CO.
LOGO DEVELOPMENT
THE SUPREME ROASTERING CO.

PACKAGING
HONDURAS
The Supreme
ROASTERING CO.
HONDURAS
SINGLE ORIGIN
HONDURAS
HONDURAS
THE SUPREME ROASTERING CO.
LABELING
THE SUPREME ROASTERING CO.

PRIMARY
SECONDARY

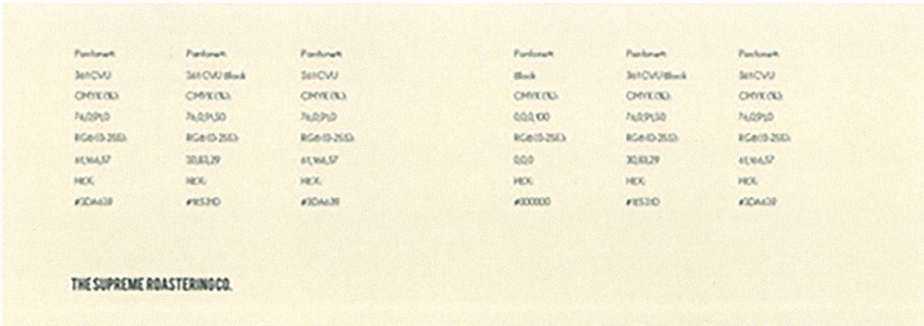
THE SUPREME ROASTERINGCO.

KENYA
SINGLE ORIGIN
PROCESSING
VARIETAL
NET 12 WT.

HONDURAS
SINGLE ORIGIN
PROCESSING
VARIETAL
NET 12 WT.

COLDBREW
THE SUPREME
Cold Brew
THE SUPREME ROASTERINGCO.

COLD BREW
KENYA
COLD BREW
COLOMBIA

The Supreme
ROASTERING CO.

COLD BREW
KENYA

The Supreme
ROASTERING CO.

BE AMAZING TODAY BUT FIRST, COFFEE
The Supreme
COLD BREW
COLOMBIA
SINGLE ORIGIN

BE AMAZING TODAY BUT FIRST, COFFEE
YOU CAN'T MAKE EVERYONE HAPPY, YOU ARE NOT COFFEE
The Supreme Roastering Co.
MAKE COFFEE NOT WAR
THERE IS ALWAYS TIME FOR COFFEE
The Supreme Roastering Co.

COLOMBIA
SINGLE ORIGIN
HONDURAS
KENYA
INDONESIA
INDIA
ETHIOPIA

INDIA
SINGLE ORIGIN
The Supreme Roastering Co.
COLOMBIA
ETHIOPIA

HONDURAS
MEDIUM ROAST
The Supreme
ROASTERING CO.
HONDURAS
SINGLE ORIGIN
HONDURAS
HONDURAS
MEDIUM ROAST

The Supreme
ROASTERING CO.
ETHIOPIA
SINGLE ORIGIN
COLOMBIA
SINGLE ORIGIN
HONDURAS
SINGLE ORIGIN

The Supreme
ROASTERING CO.
ETHIOPIA
SINGLE ORIGIN

The Supreme
ROASTERING CO.
INDIA
SINGLE ORIGIN

The Supreme
ROASTERING CO.
INDONESIA
SINGLE ORIGIN

The Supreme
ROASTERING CO.
INDONESIA
SINGLE ORIGIN

The Supreme
ROASTERING CO.
KENYA
SINGLE ORIGIN

The Supreme
ROASTERING CO.
COLOMBIA
SINGLE ORIGIN

Designed by **Uido Design Studio**

Voka

A new takeaway coffee experience for the Indian market. Voka propose to serve quality coffee at an affordable price, having a bunch of small locations all hover the major cities of India, always near the offices and most centric parts of them. Having in mind its millennial and city based customers, we designed an urban and innovative brand with a spirited and entrepreneurial identity and a bold yet sophisticated image. They wanted to look international but having their country heritage in a way Indian people can relate to it and International people can easily see where it's from.

It could be a square with arrows or it could be an elephant, if you're truly a Voka's customer, you will know it. That was the idea behind the Voka's brand mark, it's minimalist but it really catches your attention and you will have to stay staring at it to understand it. But when you see it, you will get excited and, at the same time proud of Voka, for choosing the heritage animal of India to represent their brand and all this will make you want to share it to the world.

TAKE
COF
FEE
AWAY
VOKA
VOKA
VOKA

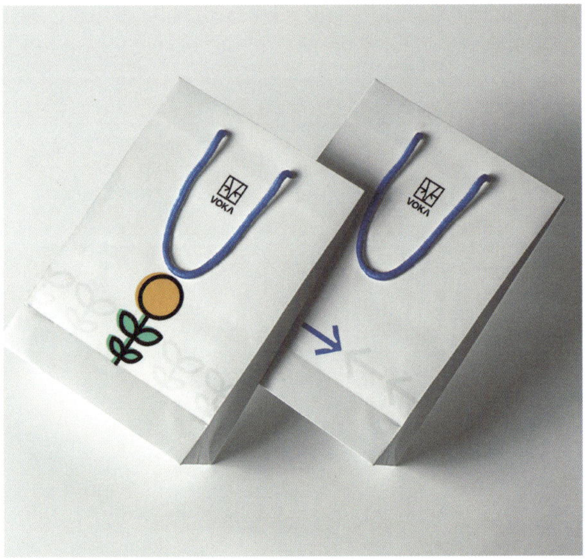

COF FEE TAKE AWAY
VOKA
It's all
<OK>

Wake up.
→ Drink a Voka.
Live your dream.

Don't
stop
your
hustle.
→
< takeaway
coffee >

'cause
everybody
deserves
quality
coffee.
VOKA

#vokastyle

Ready to start
your week?
2x1
Don't stop your Hustle
A new takeaway coffee experience

< a takeaway
were you will
ask to stay >
VOKA

Designed by ***krechet studio***

Zerno

Premium coffee house with a warm atmosphere. A place where you can feel real forget about business relax. A place of coffee moments. A logo has been developed for the project that combines the minimalism of forms (characteristic of the brand's target audience) and the smoothness of lines – a soft, friendly cafe atmosphere. The letter "o", divided into two halves, symbolizes two parts of one whole: a business person and just a living person who wants to relax over a cup of coffee.

Art-director : Tatyana Kirichenko
Designer : Serafima Toporova

место кофейных моментов
zernø
время
быть
собой
–
место
кофейных
моментов
минута
на себя –
самое
драгоцен-
ное
время

эти кофейные
мгновения,
возможно,
самые настоящие
минута
на себя –
самое
драгоцен-
ное

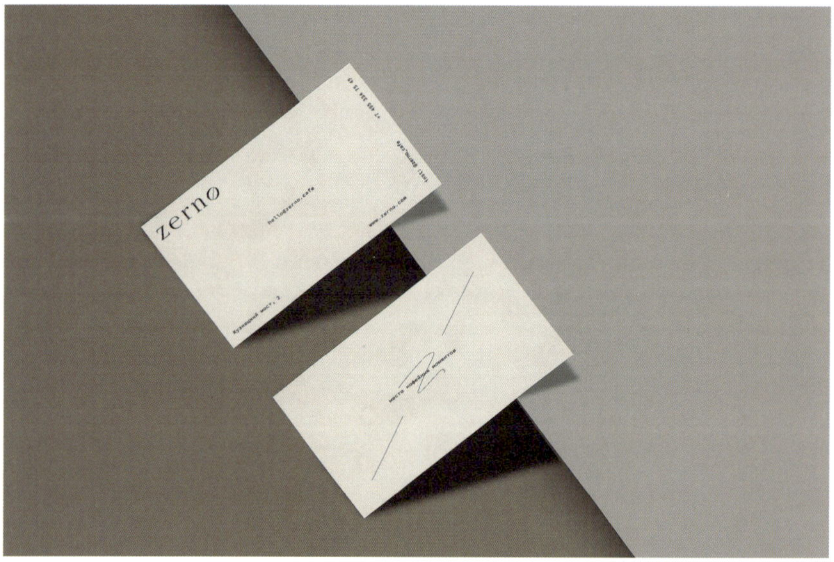
zerno
hello@zerno.cafe
www.zerno.com
Кузнецкий мост, 2

zerno

zerno

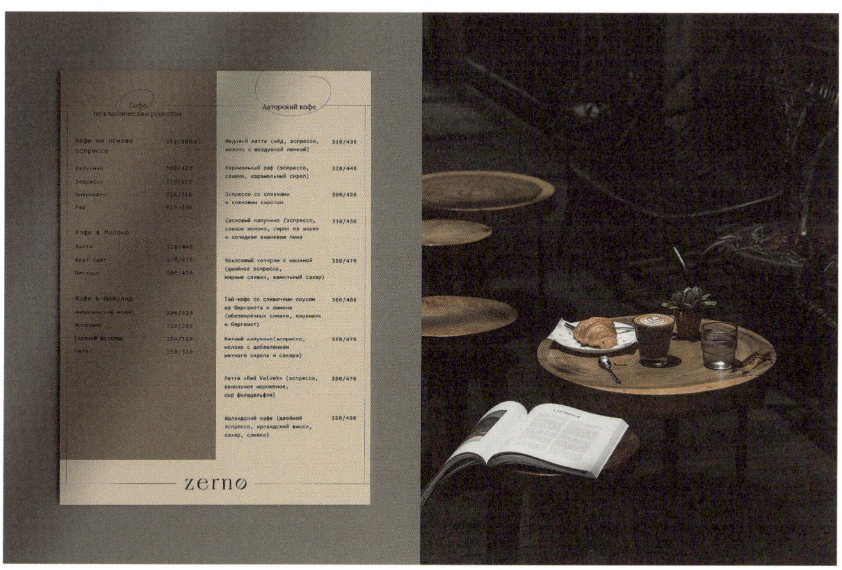
Авторский кофе
zerno

Enjoy Coffee2

Coffee Branding & Café Design

0123456789abcdefghijklmnopqrstuvwxyz

Café Design

Designed by **Red5studio**

Anh Coffee Roastery

"Anh Coffee Roastery" is a relatively new brand in the coffee market in Vietnam, not yet defined by any design style. With the current site having a good location in the center of Saigon, a large facade width, and a deep setback of the existing architectural block, this will be an advantage for Red5 to come up with good ideas for the project this time.

The story we want to tell with "Anh Coffee Roastery" is inspired by the scene of the basalt red land growing coffee on cloudy days. The feeling of being immersed in that floating place is the primary material and inspiration that Red5 wants to tell for this project.

With a current state of quite a few columns because the building was renovated from the old block, the design team connected this column system with a large common table strip spanning the entire first-floor space. Besides, creating another path outside the building leads guests from the interior space of the 1st floor to a "small outdoor garden" on the 2nd floor. Making a small atrium between the 2nd floors for planting trees is also possible to create a connection and light up the space below. With the advantage of a deeply recessed building and lots of trees, this space is suitable for those who love the natural atmosphere.

By creating a "brick red" block with the gentle curves of the white mesh system, it is difficult to know that the status quo is just a rigid glass office block. The dramatic change in colors, shapes, and materials probably creates the highlight for "Anh Coffee Roastery" at first sight.

By design language and material combination, we bring red terracotta brick from the façade into the whole interior space – floor, wall, bar or even seating blocks. The cloud part has designed by the iron grid system running on the ceiling throughout both floors and the façade. In addition, navy blue – the brand's signature color and natural wood were also cleverly incorporated into the space by the design team.

The driven by curves from the large communal table on the ground floor to the iron grid throughout the building, combined with the straight red terracotta bricks, all blend to create a fluffy sanctuary.

Design Team : Lai Chinh Truc, Nguyen Vinh Nhi, Tran Thi Kim Duyen, Lam Luong, Le Hung Thao, Pham Hoang Duy Nhan
Construction : Anh Coffee Roastery
Area : 374m^2
Location : 200 Pasteur, District 3, Saigon

anh

1ST FLOOR LAOUT PLAN

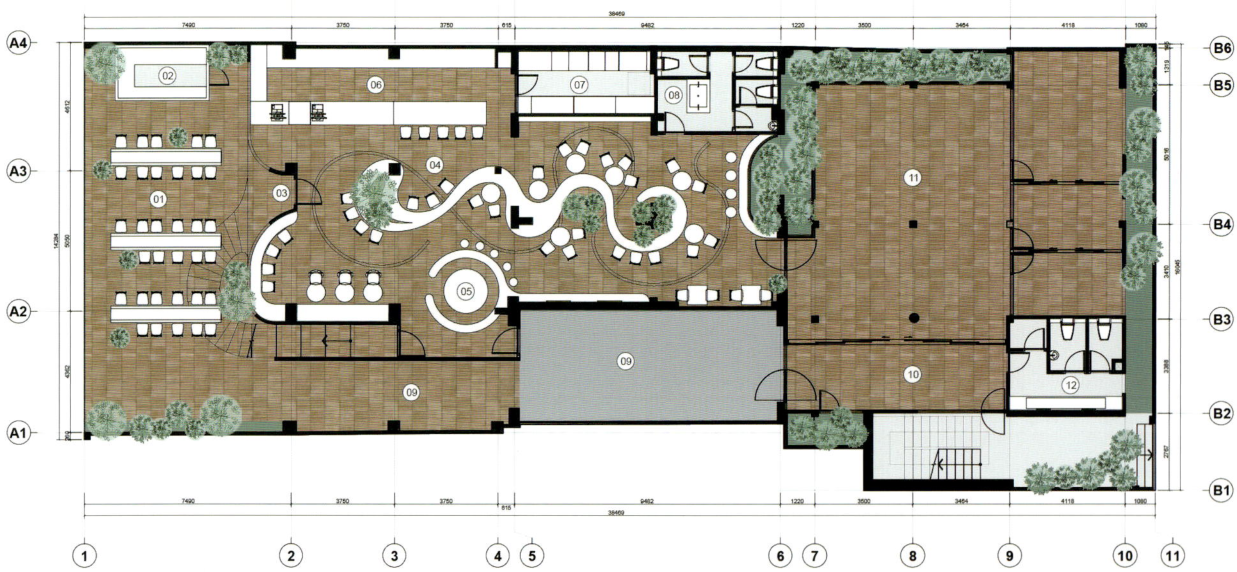

GROUN FLOOR LAOUT PLAN

01. OUTDOOR COFFEE
02. BOOTH COFFEE
03. ENTRANCE
04. INDOOR COFFEE
05. COFFEE MACHINE
06. BAR COFFEE
07. KITCHEN
08. TOILET COFFEE
09. PARKING SPACE
10. ENTRANCE CO-WORKING
11. CO-WORKING / WORKSHOP
12. TOILET CO-WORKING
13. OURDOOR COFFEE
14. CO-WORKING
15. OFFICE

BUSINESS
CENTER
PARKING

Designed by **Plainoddity**

dazzle coffe

The space was found in the dazzling experience nature, and it was decided to spatialize the wave of sunlight. I made a shadow of waves on all the walls except the window where sunlight comes in. Cylindrical acrylic was baked and crumpled, and a water shadow was created on the wall by making the light penetrating the acrylic shine toward the wall. The water shadow flowing from the line facing the ceiling makes you feel as if you are underwater. In addition, the shape of the fixtures surrounding the entire store hall was made in the shape of a connected curve to express the wave of water. With a matte material as the background, it is emphasized by using shiny materials such as acrylic or mirror steel.

Location : Bangi-dong, Songpa-gu, Seoul
Area : 34.5 m² (10.4PY)
Material / Finish : 1F – floor-bolon, wall-terrco paint, Acrylic lighting, mirror steel
Photographer : Yoong-joon Choi

dazzle

TOILET

dazzle

Designed by **Absence from island**

Duet Cafe _ Salon

It is worth noting that the barista of the cafe is indeed the Champion of Hong Kong Cup Tasters Championship 2021 organised by Hong Kong Specialty Coffee Association. It was a competition similar to wine-tasting competition that required intense sensitivity of smell, taste and eyesight as well as a lot of experience to identify the ingredients of the coffee. The client's dedication to his own specialty somehow translated into the expectation on the craftsmanship of the construction. In order to prevent a blandness of the stainless steel used, stainless steel panels of various colours and finishes have been chosen to give subtle changes on the facade and as they extend into the interior. For the washed aggregate concrete, it was widely used in Whampoa when it was originally built in the 80s, a large well-known middle-class estate in Hong Kong where the boutique is located. The exposed concrete you see now was the result after many testings on the combinations of aggregates and cement. On top of the two main elements, there is a feature rock at the shop front as well as some smaller rocks being placed inside the bar table. They are a reminder of nature as well as to remind customers the formation of coffee beans and its resulting taste indeed depends on the environment that they were grown in and was a gift from nature.

The owner of the salon is an experienced hairdresser and used to work in local salons which care a lot about speed which he dislikes. Here he wants to create a boutique salon which emphasizes the quality of the whole experience as well as the final outcome. The area of the salon can also be easily transformed into a pub-scenario where musicians can carry out mini-concrets at night and alcohol will be served as well. The infinity mirror lighting was designed to enhance the atmosphere of music nights when the rest of the lights are turned off.

Gross Built Area (m2/ ft2): 100sqm
Project Location: Whampoa , Hong Kong
Program / Use / Building Function: Cafe + Salon
Design Team: Chi, Lok Yan, Tsin, Tung, Etain
Lead Architects e-mail: chi@absencefromisland.com
*Photo Credits: 1. Absence from island 2. @f.o.v_*

DUST
WHERE COFFEE MEETS STYLE

N
SALON
(VIP ROOM)
SALON
(HAIR WASHING STATION)
SALON
CAFE
SCALE : 1:50@A3
0
1
2
3
4
5m

STORM

BEING MATERIAL

milbon

DUET

Designed by ***Plainoddity***

goon drip coffee shop

Incomplete completion, the process is soon completed. Scaffolding is a temporary structure used to support workers and materials to support the construction, maintenance, and repair of buildings, bridges and all other artificial structures. This is used during the construction process and will be demolished when the construction is complete. We wanted to dissolve the concept that the process is complete and the process is completed in the space. According to the story of the process of renewing an old bar, the scaffolding is located in the center of the space to plan the space, and in harmony with the bar, it is used as a structure to display coffee beans or pb products. In order to visualize the free hip-hop spirit, I freely drew graffiti out of the bar or framed frame and completed it. Although it is a dark old bar, it is intended to make the underground space without light rather attractive by using colorful artificial lights visible from the back of the scaffolding.

Location : Seogyo-dong, Mapo-gu, Seoul
Area : 77m² (23.3PY)
Material / Finish : Ply wood, Scaffolding, Acrylic display
Photographer : Ki-woong Hong

GOON

Move the Crowd

GOON

GOON

Move the Crowd

GOON

Designed by **Tomas Mielnikowicz**

JISU Specialty Café

Project location: Argentina – Buenos Aires – Puerto Madero
Building area (m²): 100m²
Other participants: Melko Construcciones, Paul Sende @paulSende, Monolitic.arq @monolitic, Quadri @quadribsas, Ana Zayas @zayasanai, Mercedes Risso @archisthetic
Photo credits: Hernan Taboada @ht.ph

The project was designed as a single space with quickly perceived simple lines, with pure geometries in harmony with neutral tones, stone materials, specific vegetation, and a central sculptural piece as the main lighting element. It was developed alluding to the squares of Buenos Aires, where some elements of the national and eastern culture merge with the aroma of coffee.

The site had to be endowed with a certain versatility to be able to accommodate future situations and uses that might not have been considered from the beginning. The proposal was to create a harmonious and simple space, where different uses and functions can be carried out. JISU arises from the idea of creating a brand in relation to a dynamic space, where the uses and the gastronomic offer, as well as the public and its scope, can be transformed over time, generating a multidisciplinary space, always accompanied by a rich specialty coffee.

JISU is a space for recreation, it is a moment to slow down, it is an instant in which time stops. It is a space that does not pretend to give answers, that does not pretend to condition the visitor, thus allowing contemplation and leisure, freeing the imagination, and fostering the creativity of the individual.

To achieve the reminiscence of the public spaces of the Buenos Aires centre, a decision to use one of the most seen tiles in all the squares and sidewalks of the city was made: the 64-sided tile. In this way, the visitor could subconsciously relate the sensations generated when walking on this floor to experiences that have taken place in public spaces in the open air of the city.

To emphasize the character of the square, no furniture as mobile pieces within the premises were added. Instead, benches were designed, as they are presented in the public spaces of the city, resulting in the appearance of tectonic banks, flowerpots, support sectors, and a bar. In this way, a module would appear that would configure and spatially diagram the entire project, the 40x40 cm module (size of the 64-piece tile). This pattern is present in all cafe sectors, generating a relationship between all the elements that make it up, seeking a spatial harmony governed by geometric patterns, some visible and easy to understand, others more hidden.

Another referential element used in the central Buenos Aires squares, such as Plaza de Mayo, are the golden lanterns decorated with spherical or oval lamps. From these pieces of historic urban infrastructure, the golden colour and spheric shape were incorporated into the project. The

otero.com.ar

JISU

JISU

JISU

spheres as a pure geometric figure were used to design the lighting of the bar, obtaining an artefact of simple lines with a total height of approximately three modules (120 cm), with a sphere with a diameter of half a module (20 cm), separated from each other with a distance of two modules (80 cm). The built-in golden colour of the streetlights, which is also highly visible in and quickly linked to Asian cultures, was the colour of choice for all the details of the cafe, such as baseboards, blacksmithing, light fixtures, and more.

The general spatial layout of the premises is governed by the constant link between the monolithic bar and the successive floor sectors that accompany it. Each floor sector is equivalent to a strip of a width of four modules (160cm), which could be imagined as elongated planes that fold at right angles, thus forming the different types of benches and flowerbeds in the allegorical square. Each of these strips reflects and complements the different uses of the bar.

In total eight successive strips of floor can be distinguished, perpendicular to the main axis of the bar, designed like carpets or planes of a width of four tiles, which are folded at 90 ° degrees to configure the system of benches, supports, and flowerpots. Each of these strips is separated, one from another, by a strip of round white stones. This strip fulfills several functions, in addition to allowing distinguishing the successive panels of four modules (160 cm). Each of these furrows is a four-meter linear gutter, each connected to the others, designed to guarantee good drainage and cleanliness of the premises. The selection of the round white stone connects us intuitively with Asian cultures, but at the same time, it stops the rhythm of our walk due to the change in the materiality of the soil, slowing down the speed of the usual routine, making us observe and contemplate the surrounding environment.

The central sculptural artefact is the work of artist Paul Sende. Space was opened by the architect to promote multidisciplinary work within the project, encouraging the idea of sharing and combining knowledge and disciplines, showing how different branches of art can live in harmony in the same space enriching it.

The artefact is made up of twelve concatenated quarter-circle-shaped modules. The diameter of these circular pieces coincides with the modulation of the floor panels, generating a geometric link with the genesis module of the cafe floor. The artefact of curved lines stands out for its morphological composition, contrasting with the rigidity of the right angles of the space that contains it, but at the same time, it maintains a geometric relationship with the surrounding whole.

All its modules are programmed and connected to each other, achieving a static lighting position with adjustable power, plus a total of six different lighting sequences, resulting in a very attractive movement of lights, which at times manages to recreate the passage of clouds under the sun, moving us to a possible situation experienced outdoors.

<u>Words from the founder of JISU</u>

"Our original intention to open JISU was inspired by Jeju Island in South Korea which we liked a lot during previous trips. It is an island of paradisiacal nature located in the middle of the great metropolises of Asia. Jeju is surrounded by an almost black blue sea and filled with Jeju oranges, oranges native to the island.

After countless searches and also recommended through friends, we finally found Tomas, a young architect with a powerful, exquisite, concise design style and an extremely concentrated and thoughtful personality. Upon receiving the finished project, after injecting its clear, mature and balanced architectural style into this place, we were pleasantly surprised. We discovered that Mini Jeju Island has become a JISU Island, which is totally new and fantastic, which does not exist anywhere else in the world. Thanks to the full respect for our original ideas and with the aura of Tomas, the new JISU space is sweet, fresh and clear. It always brings our visitors a feeling of happiness and amazement for what is new. Even the most discreet corner can be a source of inspiration for photographers and a good place to take a photo.

We sincerely hope that the future development of JISU can always be accompanied by Tomas and the spirit of his design. We look forward to some time that JISU can offer a wonderful, unique and refreshing experience to all of you too."

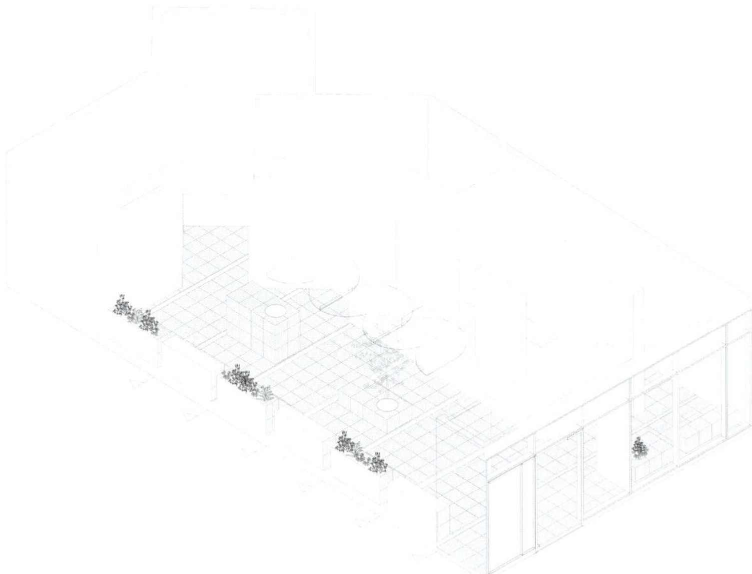

JISU

JISU

JISU

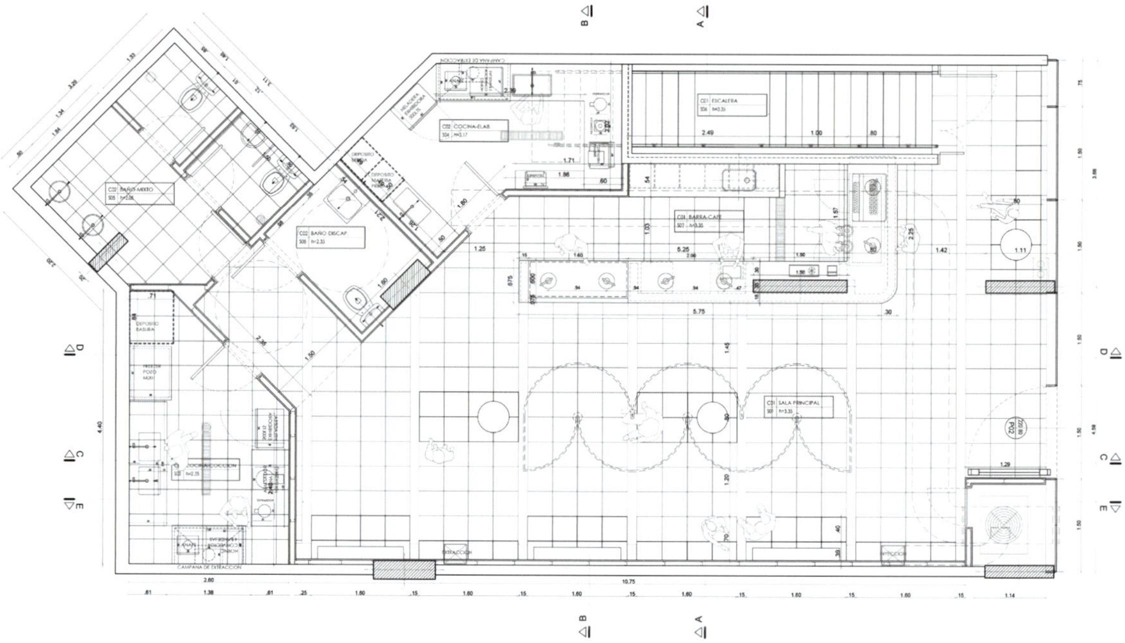

JISU

JISU

JISU

PIDA
AQUI
RETIRE
AQUI
JISU

VENTA
RETIRO

Designed by **Plainoddity**

KAUFFF ROASTERS

A compound word of KAUF, which means 'sell' in German, and the letters FF from coffee.

Super Mart and Super Mario

- *A supermart*

All the ceilings and walls are removed only leaving the necessary furniture placed on the remaining bases. The furniture is displayed like an angled cabinet; the method a market displays goods, making the whole space look like an image. When first entering the bar area, you can see a space formed of repeated angles. The back of the bar is an island bar that acts as a workbench for the Baristas to make drip coffee and a place where they can communicate with the customers. Using the angle-type configuration allows easy adjustment of the height of spaces of storage. The roasting room is made with glass walls, showing visitors the process of the coffee roasting. An angle post is set up to display coffee beans on sale. Bricks and boxes with the "Kaufff" logo, to cover the messy parts inside the roasting room.

- *The exterior looks like a castle from Super-Mario*

The old bricks make the whole place look like a castle from Super Mario. The inside also has a similar theme. Chairs and shelves are made with bricks. In addition, water droplet marks from Super Mario are on, where the drip coffee is made, and coin marks are on the top of the bar. A cart full of coffee beans and packaging boxes is also displayed to give visitors an image that this place is full of products. We decorated the space with cactus for inner plants.

Location : Samseong-dong, Gangnam-gu, Seoul
Area : 113.7m² (34.4PY)
Material / Finish : Exposed concrete, Mart display rack, channel furniture, brick, lpm table, plastic box display
Photographer : Ki-woong Hong

KAUF(FF)

KAUFFF ROASTERS KAUFFF ROASTERS

KAUFFF ROASTERS
BASED IN SEOUL

ROASTERS
KO(FF)EE ROASTING

KAUF

KAUF

KAUF

(FF)

KAUF(FF)

서강

Designed by ***Red5studio***

Okkio Caffe

Okkio Caffe is a chain of coffee shops that has 2 branches in the market. With the purpose of making the difference but still keeping the spirit of youth, our design team has chosen red for the building - the color will not only identify the brand but also bring out the retro-spirit that the construction is aimed at. Vuong Gia Ve is an influential and inspiring director for the Okkio Caffe, so this design story was inspired by the movie "2046" - his famous film is about the return train from 2046.

Based on that idea, the building's façade is designed as the train's windows with the iron bars as the highlight. Additionally, the ceiling inside is built up with the curved shape as the train's one.

Moreover, the "frame in frame" is decorated by the idea of getting the natural light from the windows, the ceilings, etc straight to the floor. Our design team wants to emphasize the prominent points here, which are the counter and the ceilings' system of the building.

Together with the brand's traditional materials such as old bricks and coppers, which bring a friendly and warm environment like usual, we want to introduce other materials which are more modern like the paint gradient effect, and the poly ceiling style. Besides the retro style like Vuong Gia Tue's movie, we also use the red color from the grinding wheel surface...

If Okkio is a train, the timeline will be the colors changing effects and. Our design team will focus on the Led HUE light system which is put at the bar corner. The light color is going to change differently at different times of the day.

The light system is also an emphasis of Okkio Xuan Thuy. In the morning, it will be delighted as the natural light which is runs along the side of the ceiling's hole. At night, Okkio is going to be warm, romantic and private enough for the customers which the light will mainly focus on the bar corner instead.

If people have a chance to observe Okkio in the lively sunset, you will be definitely impressed by the peaceful red building with tons of light moving like a movie from the future that comes back to the past.

Design Team : Lai Chinh Truc, Nguyen Vinh Nhi, Tran Quoc Huy
Area : 70m^2
Location : 110 Xuan Thuy Street, District 02, Saigon
Photographer : Đo Sy

OKKIO

OKKIO

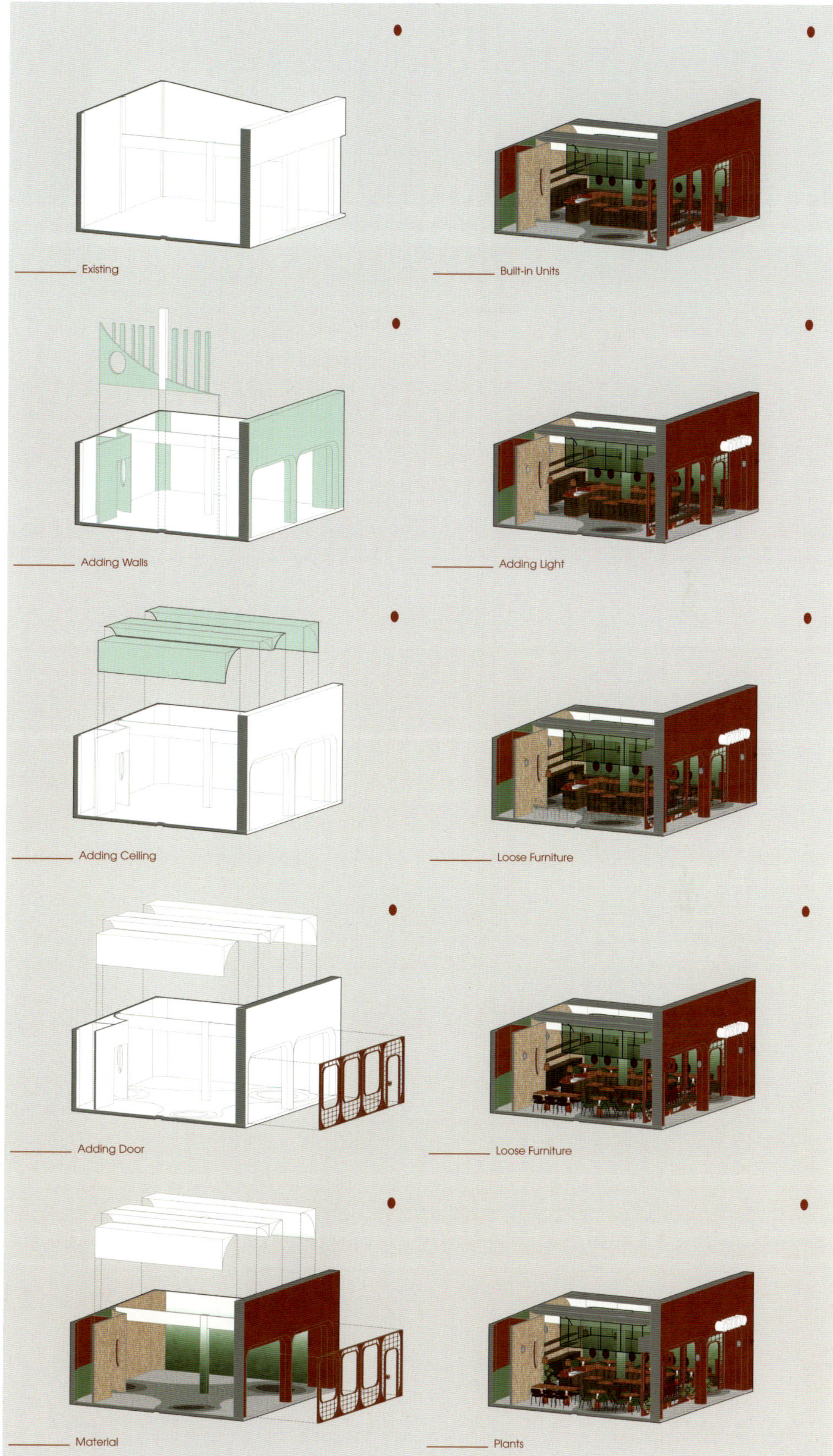
Existing
Built-in Units
Adding Walls
Adding Light
Adding Ceiling
Loose Furniture
Adding Door
Loose Furniture
Material
Plants

OKKIO

OKKIO

OKKIO

OKKIO

Designed by **Plainoddity**

Peer Coffee Roasters

Coffee that blooms next to Gwanghuimun, the history of the Joseon Dynasty (four 小門). In this place where old and low buildings are lined up, Peer Coffee Roasters is designed as a comfortable space that is comfortable and accessible to people rather than being an unusual and special space. The old exterior and the internal wooden structure were not demolished but were remodeled to compensate for the old places.

On the first floor, windows were made for communication with passers-by and for take-out guests, and old materials were exposed to the outside, giving a familiar and comfortable image. To bring the historical background of Gwanghuimun, a counter and a service table were made in the shape of a dwi-ju (a bin that holds grains made of wood).

Climbing through a narrow staircase leads to a wide open second floor by exposing the wooden ceiling. The first floor is a place to stay for a while, and the second floor is designed so that group guests can sit comfortably.

Location : Gwanghuimun, Sindang-dong, Jung-gu, Seoul
Area : 71 m² (1F 30 m² / 2F 41 m²)
Material / Finish : 1F – tile, wall-paint, facade-reused, antique old wood flooring / 2F – Ceiling Wood Structure Exposed, stained veneer, stepping stone granite, BOLON
Photographer : Ki-woong Hong(kiwoong.cfc@gmail.com)

PEER
123

Designed by **Still Young**

M stand_ SHANGHAI BFC

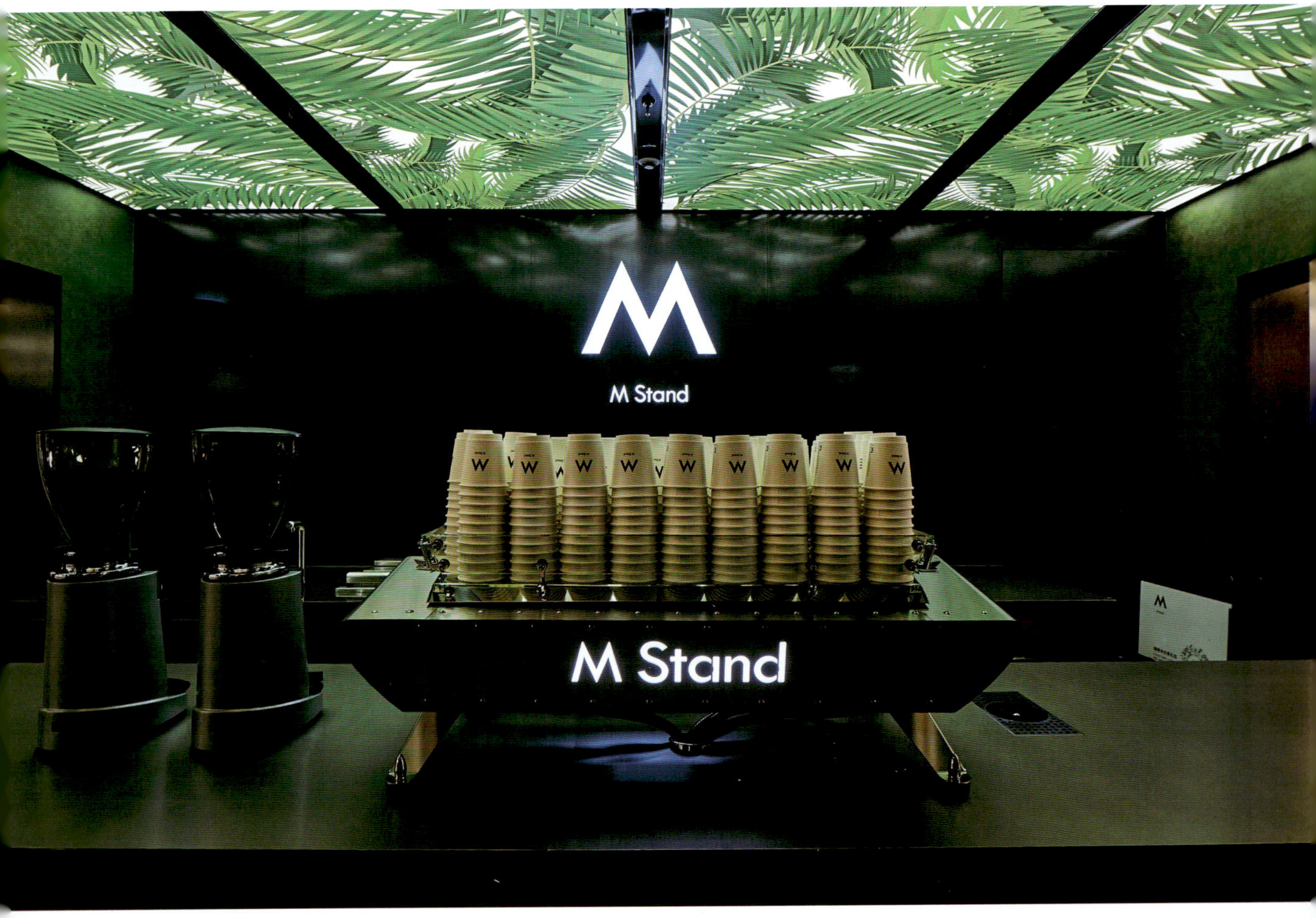

M Stand

M Stand

M Stand

M Stand
M Stand

M Stand
M Stand

M
M Stand

M
M Stand

M Stand

M Stand

M Stand

M Stand
M Stand
M Stand

Designed by **design by 83**

SINKI HAERO

Singihaero, designed by Busan based 'design by 83', is located next to the southernmost area of Geoje island.

A good space to us should be more than simply delivering an image. It also needs to provide the nuances, atmosphere, scenery and sights of the place to those who stay. We tried to design with the hope that it would be a quiet but powerful space where anyone can enjoy the experience of relaxation and appreciation.

Singihaero is a bakery and coffee shop located in front of the calm sea in Dadaeri village in the southern part of Geoje island. We tried capture the horizontal beauty of the sea along with the calm and peaceful atmosphere of this place by emphasizing the linear elements through the cool feeling of unique and edges without unnecessities.

In order to express a simple and horizontal furniture design that does not interfere with the landscape, we tried to express so that the horizontal and linear elements can be emphasized by combining different physical properties horizontally and vertically with a light and unique feeling.

You can enjoy the sea no matter where you sit, and you can enjoy the sea view, and the layout of the space gives you a feeling of relaxation. Using warm wood and soft fabrics, it provides both visual and functional comfort at the same time.

By using objects that have curves and edges resembling the flexibility of waves, we designed a place that provides comfort and enjoyment away from everyday life.

Interior design: Min suk Kim, Dong hyun Nam, Chan un Park
Space styling & furniture : Min suk Kim, Kang Ji-yeon
Location : 41, Dadae 5-gil, Nambu-myeon, Geoje-si, Gyeongsangnam-do
Area : 492m^2
Photographer : Dong kyu Kim

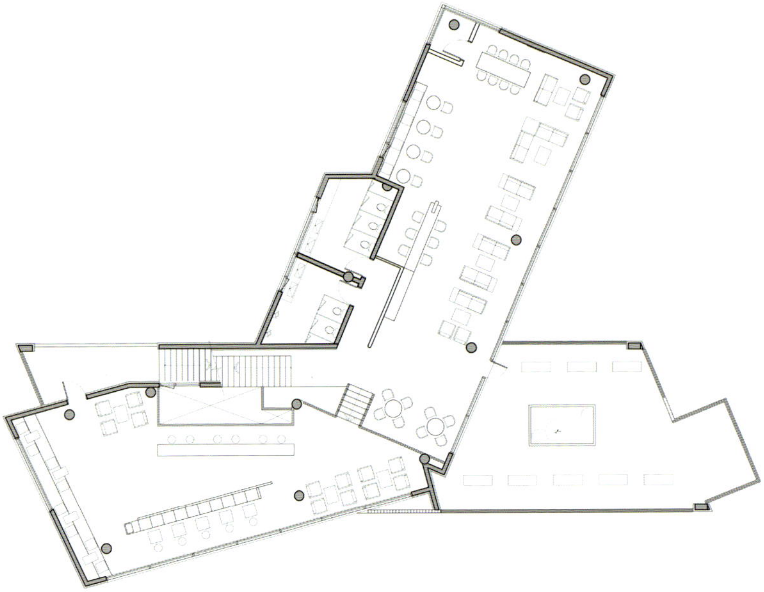

2nd Floor

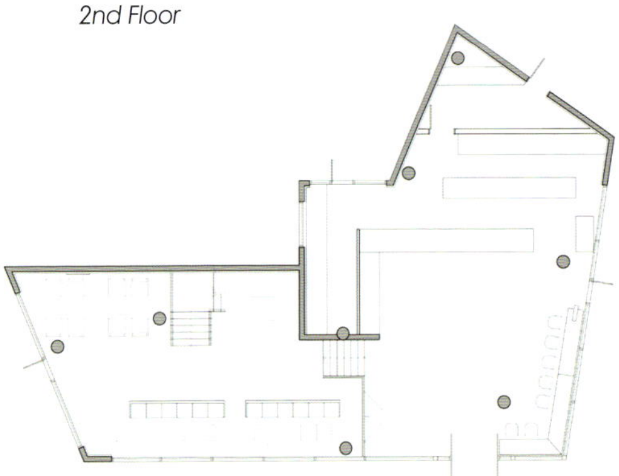

1st Floor

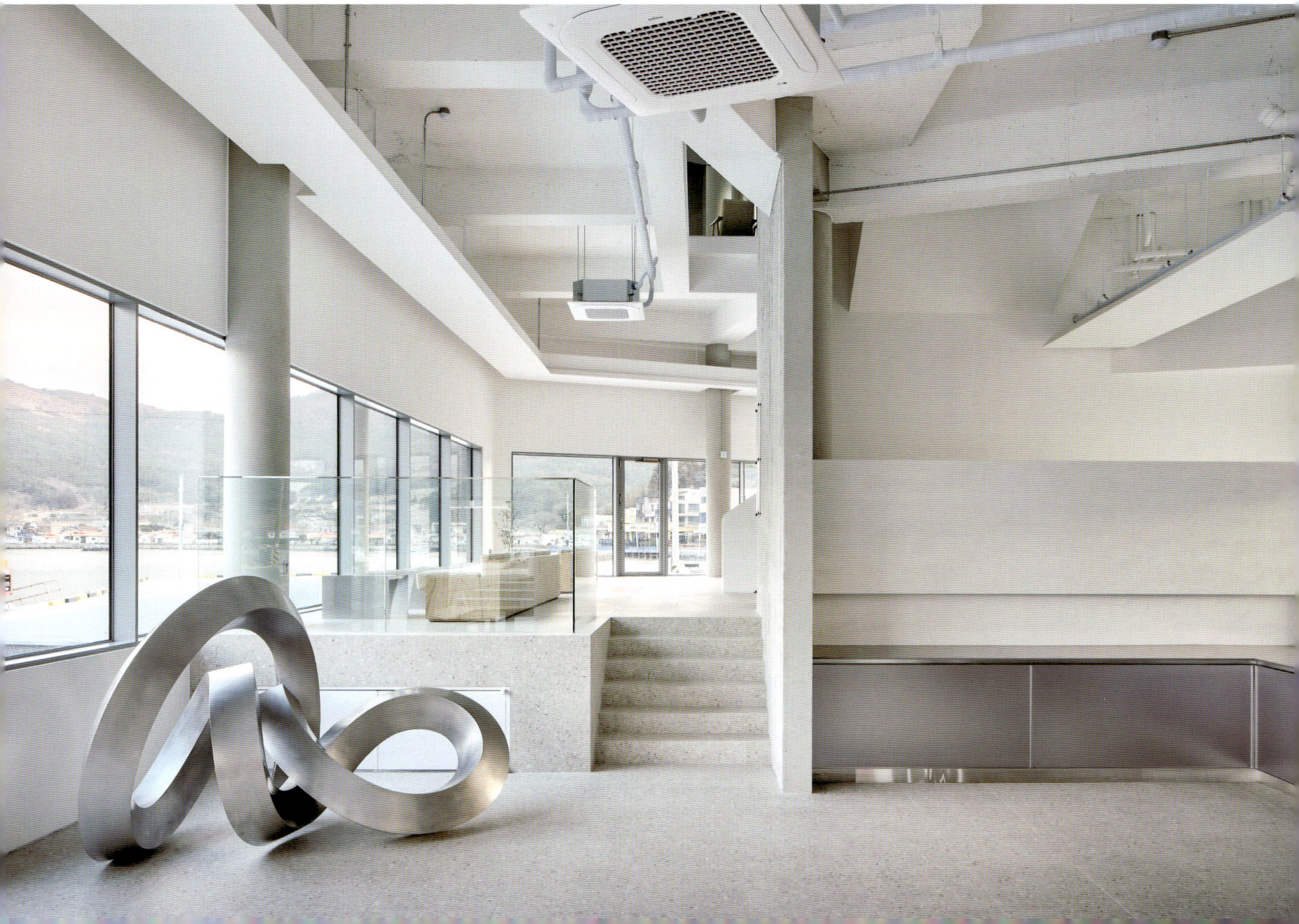

BAKING ROOM

Designed by **design by 83**

SSAP Coffee

INTERIOR

Designed by studio "designby83," based in Busan, Korea, SSAP offers pastries and coffee and is located next to Ulsan's Grand Park.

The client asked us for a vintage and hip space. We tried to convey a space where the history and traces of the original space can coexist. Unlike conventional vintage and hip images, we came up with our own interpretation of the space including sustainability.

Despite the passage of time, we thought about the design with hopes that it would last and continue to deepen. In the process of demolishing the interior of the interior space, consisting of exposed rough concrete walls, worn-out floor tiles, cold metal windows and simple glass windows, almost all structural elements were intentionally left intact.

The interior space is put together so that you can feel the natural changes of concise and physical properties by including relaxed arrangements and artificial decorations as much as possible. It creates a two-sided and harmonious atmosphere with the intention to feel visual comfort and cynicism simultaneously within the vertical line of warm wood and metal.

It is also designed to form an organic relationship with this space form acrylic lighting. The cafe uses a focal color of red for cabinets, chairs, bakery showcases, and raceways, where minor electric circuits pass. This takes into account the sensibility of the MZ generation, which is characterized by pursuing an unusual experience different from the existing trend, and at the same time, maintaining the familiarity and comfort for those who remember this place.

The exterior is created so that it blends with the original old red brick. It emphasizes the neatness of the facade's expansion of the horizontal long rectangular space and visually separates it with wood adding depth, and metal–a material that is unlikely to change.

The main door where customers come in and the heavy doors installed for ventilation are made of zinc steel sheets. In addition, the windows with visible inside are closed with regular intervals of birch plywood, so that the inside atmosphere is naturally harmonized.

We designed this place to have a vibe unique to SSAP by unifying the relationship between the interior and the exterior space (form/texture/color/ atmosphere).

FURNITURE

Tt(Thanks to) is a lifestyle design studio. We design objects from experiences within the nature and everyday surroundings. The natural beauty from various materials and the Concerns about sustainability us to our endless creativity. As time goes by, I hope that it will be someone's fun life beyond valuable products.

The "SSAP" furniture focuses on its properties and characteristics, which is represented through the use of materials. made only in a prefabricated manner to express the beauty brought by precise and delicate dot, line, and shape. approached the design with concerns about materials and fastening methods, and I was inspired by the assembly method of wood furniture. The surface of the furniture was finished differently to maximize the rough texture and cold lines brought by the material.

Project : SSAP(STAY SWEET AT PLACE) COFFEE

Design : Min suk Kim, Dong hyun Nam, Chan un Park

Design Team : Su hyun Jo

Construction : Se hyun Lee

Furniture : Chan un Park x TT / Byung min Bae

Location : 1F, 10-3, Daegongwon-ro 207beon-gil, Nam-gu, Ulsan, Republic of Korea

Area : 96m^2

Wall material : Painting, terra coat, aluminum plate, zinc steel sheets, artificial leather, veneer, birch plywood, tile

Ceiling material : Concrete Polishing, Painting, zinc steel sheets, birch plywood

Floor material : Concrete Polishing, Tile

Photographer : Dong kyu Kim

SSAP

SSAP

SSAP

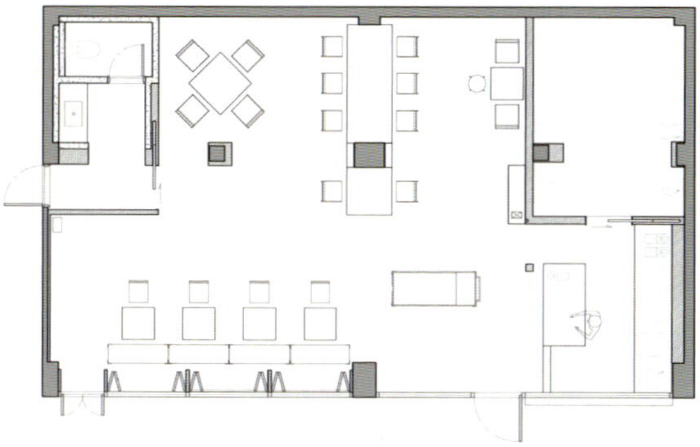

1st Floor

Designed by **YRAD**

Takenishi Terrace Coffee Shop

This is a project that confronts to the nature of the renewal of land use after a deteriorating rental building facing a shopping street was demolished.

The site is in the centre of Oita City, on the western edge of the oldest shopping street in the area. The bustle of the past has faded and the arcade has turned into a place that people just pass through to get somewhere else. We received a request from a client who runs a letting agency in the town to use a corner of the site where a car park was going to be built after the building was demolished for a small tenant space and a place for people to go such as a park where they can take a break, in order to bring the bustle back to the area.

We had the image of the tenants being people who would liven up ordinary everyday life as an extension of routine.
In addition, the front façade sandwiched in the arcade includes wazawaza Building*[1], a complex owned by the same client; connecting the two facilities together was one of the requests to liven up the area.

We perceived that the presence of tenants who would liven the place up with a share awareness with the builder was indispensable in creating a space that attracts people and we believed that it was best to determine the tenants in advance of proceeding with the project to create a cooperative space. Further, although the construction is small, it was possible to create multiple shops and various indoor and outdoor spaces for a diverse, lively experience.

The three shops that signed up came to fruition and were given accessibility and we investigated the careful positioning of fixtures to encourage the movement of customers from one shop to another. The earth that we removed during excavation when demolishing the building was not put back in its original position and, taking advantage of its shape, we created a closed-in and calm shared space. The space in front of the shops where people can casually drop by and the terrace seats where they can feel the changing seasons enhance the quality of the public space that anyone can visit easily.

Keeping rainfall in the shopping street to a minimum while breaking up the arcade and buildings delivers a bright and airy shopping street. The front and the back are linked through the buildings. They invite people who are curious to pass through and are an opportunity to casually stop and look.

The alley that was created in the process of extending and reconstructing wazawaza Building was incorporated

into the building and the alley that passes through the two buildings plays the role of drawing out the attractiveness of this area.

Several months have passed since construction was completed and you can clearly feel that the flow and number of people who visit this area have changed.
This place has reactivated the flow of people and we think that we would like to engage with it positively beyond just the framework of design to give hope to our current unease.

[1] wazawaza Building(WZ bldg.) : Completed in 2009 and designed by Takao Shiotsuka of Takao Shiotsuka Atelier

Architects : Ryosuke Enomoto, Yuuki Tanaka / YRAD
Location : Oita, Japan (3-6-12, Chuo-machi, Oita-city, Oita, JAPAN, 870-0035)
Usage : Store (Complex store)
Structural engineering : Kuroiwa Structural Engineers.co.,ltd
Construction : PAS.co.,ltd
Client : Shinoitatochi.co.,ltd
Garden design : Original Botanica
Sign + Graphic design : Yuuki Tanaka / YRAD
Structure : Wood
Site area : 237.51m²
Building area : 87.63m²
Total floor area : 64.38m²
Photographer : Toshiyuki Yano

plan

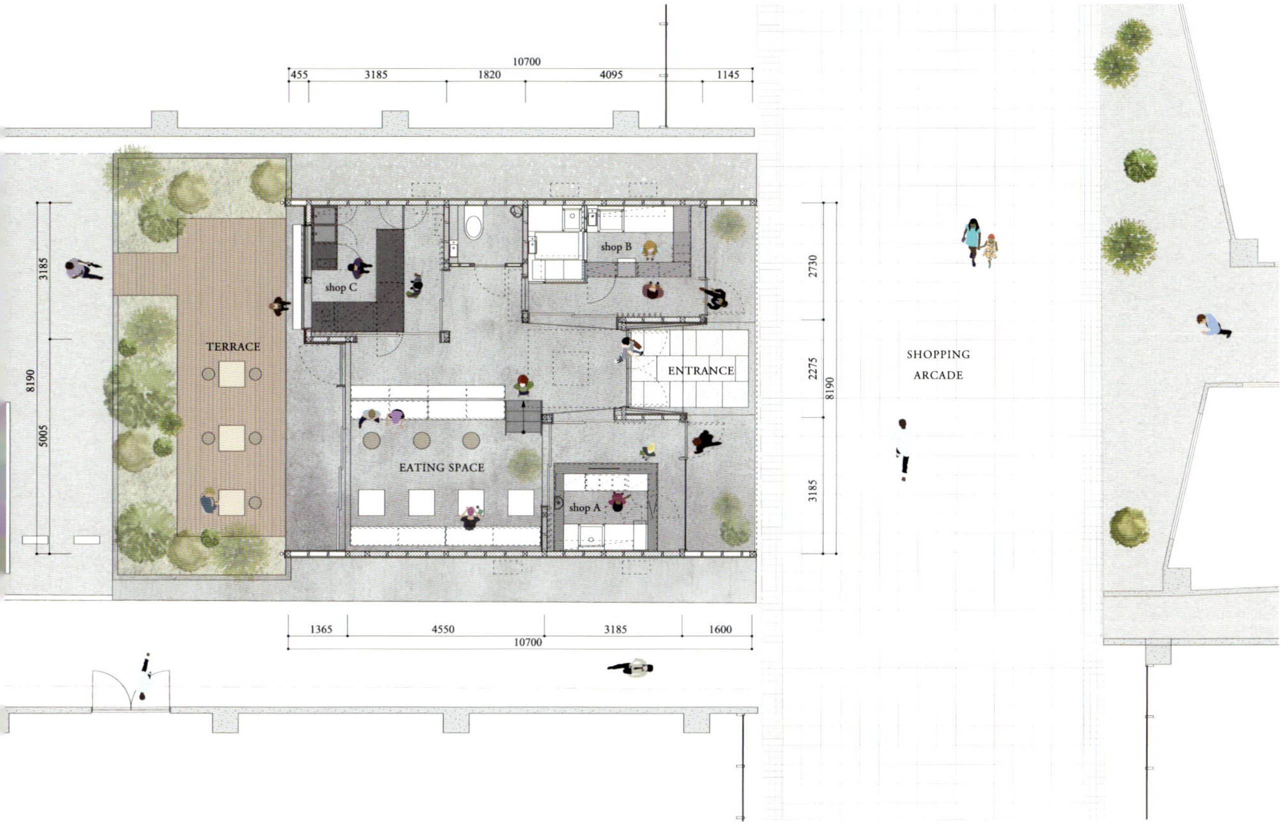
10700
455
3185
1820
4095
1145
TERRACE
shop C
shop B
ENTRANCE
EATING SPACE
shop A
SHOPPING
ARCADE
3185
8190
5005
2730
2275
8190
3185
1365
4550
3185
1600
10700

TAKENISHI TERRACE
wazawaza

TAKENISHI TERRACE

RISING HOPE
2021

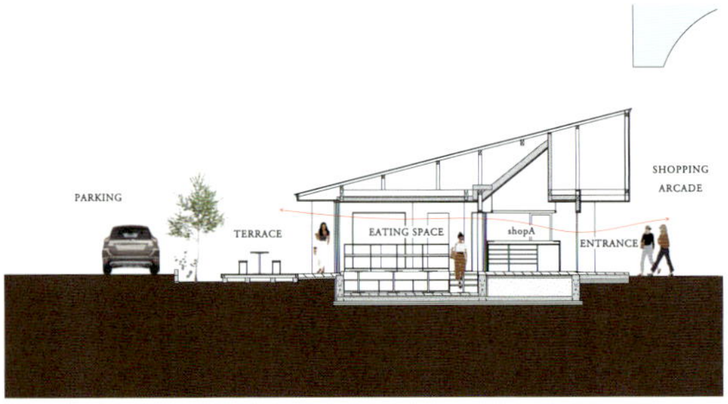

section 01

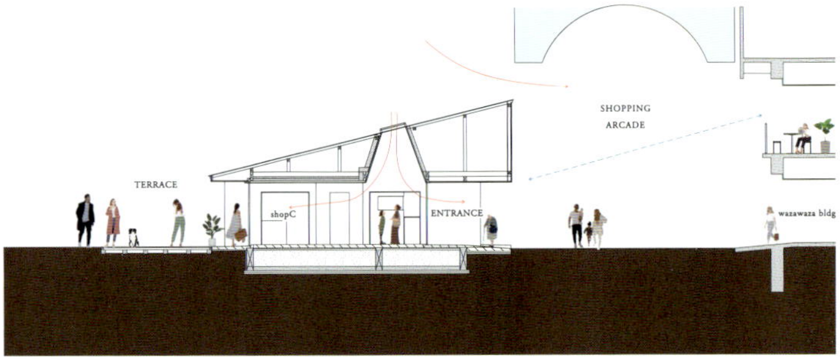

section 02

nico
ドーナツ

nico
TODAY'S FLAVORS

hello.goodbye

Designed by **Absence from island**

Today is Long Café

Gross Built Area (m2/ ft2): 30sqm
Project Location: Sai Ying Pun , Hong Kong
Program / Use / Building Function: Cafe
Design Team: Chi, Etain
Lead Architects e-mail: chi@absencefromisland.com
Photo Credits: 1. Absence from island 2. @f.o.v_ 3@lizeatery 4@dypiem

The clients were a group of individuals who have studied and worked separately in Australia and have subsequently moved back to hometown Hong Kong where they eventually met due to a shared passion for coffee. One of them has become a well-accomplished barista and another has become a successful public-relation manager. The cafe is a place to house their fond memories of Australia and the good coffee that makes their life, which they would very much like to share with local residents and to make the cafe into a social hub.

They named the Cafe as "Today Is Long" (TIL) and the design was inspired by the golden sunset of Australia. Warm red-orange became the theme colour which it also took reference from the sandstone monolith - Uluru in the Red Centre of Northern Australia. The texture of the baked earthy sandstone is also represented by the fired ceramic tiles anchored at the lower part of the facade.

The hemisphere of setting sun has been applied in various ways on the facade. This helped form a facade with a strong geometrical language which distinguishes the cafe from its surroundings of old buildings. It allows the cafe to stand out and be noticed. One of the hemispheres became the welcome arch at the entrance which formed a short tunnel to transport customers from the hustle and bustle in Sai Ying Pun to the quiet and comfortable interior. Another formed a recessed wall pattern for the take-away counter. The third hemisphere was rotated sideway and formed the largest window to bring in as much natural light as possible. Apart from the facade, there was one full final circle in the interior which formed as the backdrop for the seating area.

富豪燒臘

Australia has always been blessed with abundant amounts of sunlight, thus a lot of white colour has been used together with the large windows to enhance the bright and airy atmosphere. And spaces have been reserved under the entrance arch, seating area and the overhead storage for plantings in order to create a green, lush and natural environment. Coffee grain used in the cafe will also be recycled as fertilisers for the plantings.

Sai Ying Pun, given its proximity to the University of Hong Kong, has been famous for its mix of locals and foreigners in recent years. And the idea of the cafe being a social hub is expressed by the seating arrangement - bench seating has been fitted in one triangular corner of the shop with the two rows facing each other. With the benches and the coffee counter arranged along the periphery of the cafe and with a focal point in the centre, the arrangement shall enhance interaction and create a sense of community. A thin bar table has also been designed on the facade for customers, especially dog-owners, to enjoy their coffee outdoors and to look into the cafe at the same time.

EXIT 出口
ESPRESSO 30
LONG BLACK 35
MAC
PICCOLO
FLAT WHITE 40
LATTE
CAP
MAGIC 40
LMTU
DIRTY
FANCY 45
DRIP 50
COLD BREW 65

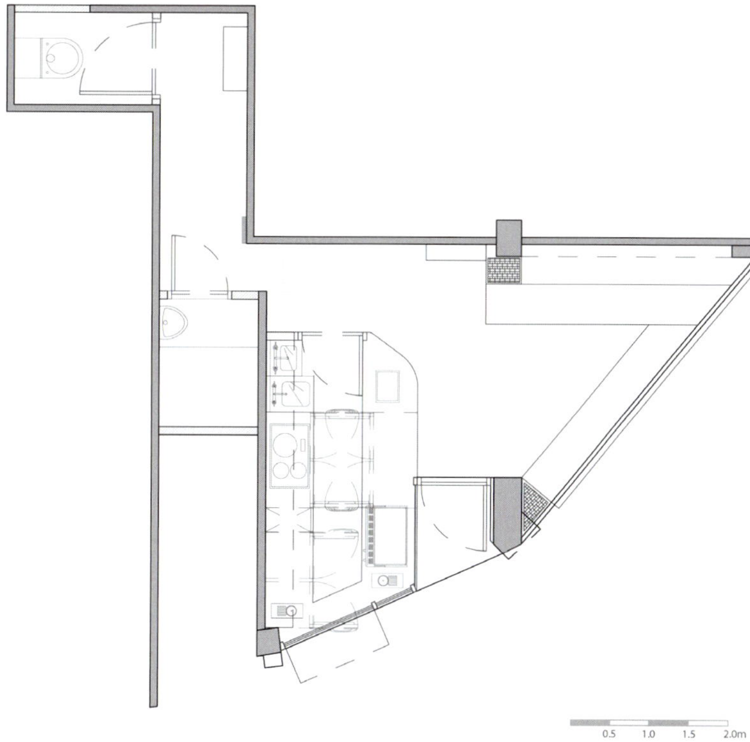
0.5
1.0
1.5
2.0m

TIL
Food
MENU

Professional Beauty

TODA

S L NG

Designed by **Still Young**

M stand_ WUHAN Garden RD

M
M Stand

M Stand
M Stand
JOIN US
M Stand

M Stand
M Stand
M Stand
M Stand

M Stand

M Stand
灭火器

M Stand

M Stand

M Stand

stop wishing start doing
stop wishing start doing
stop wishing start doing
stop wishing start doing

Designed by **Still Young**

M stand_
WUHAN International Plaza 2#

M Stand

M Stand

M Stand

M Stand
stop wishing start doing
stop wishing start doing
stop wishing start doing
stop wishing start doing

M Stand
M Stand

M Stand
MSTAND

stop wishing start doing
stop wishing start doing
stop wishing start doing
stop wishing start doing

stop wishing start doing
stop wishing start doing
stop wishing start doing
stop wishing start doing

M
M Stand

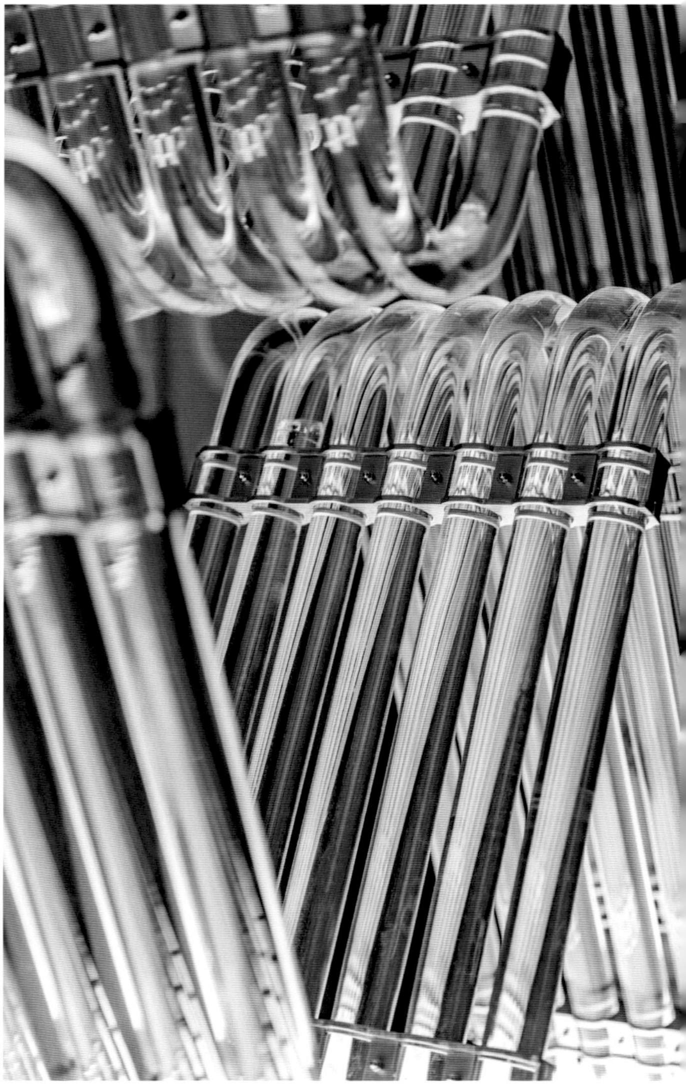

Designed by **Still Young**

M stand_ WUHAN GUANGGU K11

Stand

M Stand
M Stand

M Stand

M Stand

M Stand
M Stand

stop wishing
stop wishing
stop wishing
M Stand

Participation
Designers

0123456789abcdefghijklmnopqrstuvwxyz

Absence from Island p.234 / p.336

Absence from Island collaborated with Studio Etain Ho

Studio Background / Absence from island is an award-winning practice founded in 2020 by Tang Chi Chun, collaborated with Etain from Studio Etain Ho. Its work is a direct reflection of the partners' upbringing in Hong Kong and their work experience in Madrid and London.

Within the last two years, Absence from island has quickly gained recognition both locally and internationally. Our work has been published by SCMP, dezeen, designboom, archdaily, AD Clever, detail magazine etc. and has been featured in the book titled "Never Too Small". The Studio has also won numerous awards within its short establishment, including the INSIDE Award of World Festival of Interiors and Good Design Award 2021 in Japan.

Studio Philosophy / Hong Kong is a fast-paced city, famous for its efficiency and economic success. Despite its high density, it is also blessed with nature. Hong Kong, our hometown, is no doubt a bustling city and more importantly, it is a beautiful city full of hidden breathing spaces. Regardless of our project locations, our design philosophy will always be a reflection of the city's persona.

Tang Chi Chun

Etain Ho

Min suk Kim
Dong hyun Nam
Chan un Park

design by 83 p.300 / p.310

- We believe that the ultimate goal of space design is for better space use. -

design by 83 is not designed to demonstrate the capabilities of the designer himself. We will fully understand the characteristics of space and create space with a clear concept through analysis. It is our mission to create a space where the user can feel comfortable and happy.

Branding / It gives branding and space design connectivity to clearly communicate brand awareness to consumers. Common design, not just the same design as I saw "only you" I try to make your own brand.

Interior / Designs all spaces where people's actions, such as commerce, office work, medical care, and residential space, take place. The commercial space allows you to feel brand identity in the space, and makes it a comfortable and practical space in residential space. I want to gather good people, create a good space and create a good culture.

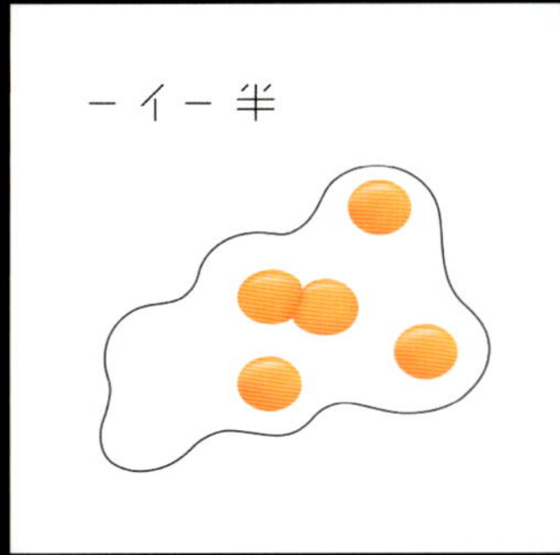

kongsi design p.132

We kongsi ideas ;
We share different perspectives and aesthetics
We kongsi tangan ;
We get our hands dirty in conceptual and experimental processes
We kongsi watak ;
We own a personality that is both quirky and dreamy
We kongsi dream ;
We are two halves that make a whole

Tatyana Kirichenko

Krechet Studio p.050 / p.062 / p.202

Hi, I'm Tanya, art director with a technical background and founder of Krechet Studio. For more than 7 years, my main task has been to develop visual communication between the brand and its audience, creating an emotionally charged contact between them using identity and animation.

low key

low key Design p.034 / p.054 / p.164 / p.180

low key Design is an independent design studio based in Shanghai. Our graphics open the door for brands to connect with people.

Marka Works p.068 / p.088 / p.114 / p.170 / p.190

I have been dealing with graphic design and various sub-branches for about 15 years. In this process, I have worked with many global and local brands. For 5 years, we have been creating great brands under the name of MarkaWorks and helping brands transform. During this time, we had the opportunity to work on over 200 projects from 25 different countries. We continue our projects globally and continue to inspire millions of creatives on social media and various design platforms. I've designed brand identities and other branding elements for clients like Google, Turkish Airlines, Vision Healthcare. I must also proudly say that I created the visual identities of the Caffeinication, Cey Natural Foods, GreenWhey, Spout, Milksta, Trive, Bloomy, Las Habitas, Be So Happy, Alicis, Shakeplus, Herbaly, Cat Turner, Capeesh and Fluxus brands. In addition to all these projects, I enjoy working with small businesses and start-ups whose projects I believe in. I support them in achieving their big dreams. With my agency MarkaWorks, we become long-term solution partners and companions of our clients. We see their success as our own. And that's why we always focus on giving the best. Me and my agency MarkaWorks have been featured in numerous magazines, books and online publications. We have also won awards many times in various fields and platforms. The brand identity projects that I have prepared are shown as examples by Adobe on the pages that explain the importance of brand identity.

Mustafa Akülker

Monga Design p.128

We're a 24H/D brazilian design studio that wants to work with good people who are willing to respect our process and understand that valuing people makes the journey enjoyable and the result better.

plainoddity p.224 / p.242 / p.262 / p.284

"new nuance from ordinary ones."

plainoddity is creating a new atmosphere in everything around us that we have become accustomed to and have missed. A unique atmosphere is created by adding a design approach called "oddity" to the "Plain" of objects and spaces.PlainOdity covers all areas of design, construction, and supervision, from space to furniture.

Red5studio p.208 / p.272

Red5studio is an Interior design firm based in Saigon, which specializes in residential, apartment, retail, hospitality, and commercial practices. We provide a full-service that starts from the concept development to the final construction. Red5studio was founded by Interior Designer Lai Chinh Truc.

Sabhat KK Rak p.156

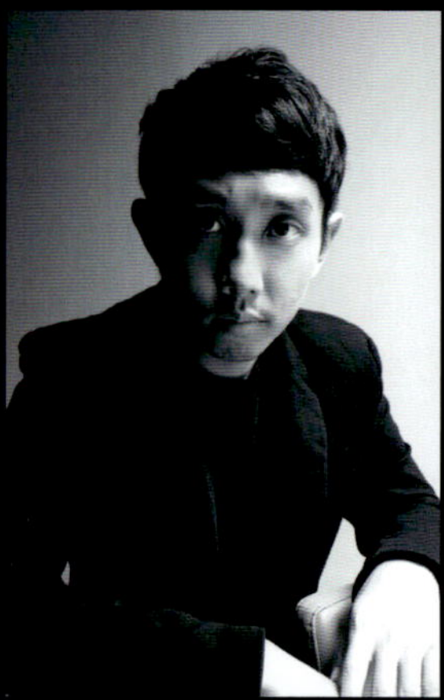

Sabhat KK Rakitawan – a Creative Director based in Bangkok, Thailand. He specializes in branding, identity and graphic design with an understanding in business development. A visual storyteller, critical thinker with a passion for simple yet meaningful designs, he offers his clients iconic branding solutions. His storytelling breathes life into every design, brands and products. This is seen throughout his various body of works. He helps his clients achieve their visions by laying down strong foundations for their brand's identity and through crafting exceptional design, storytelling and stores experiences. Balancing conceptual storytelling along with business development is his key to execute successful projects.

Serena Studio p.080

We are a design studio that creates concepts and develops ideas for people and brands through artisanal design and conceptual thinking. We are obsessed with simplification and details, but above all we are passionate about what we do.

We are specialists in brand creation and strategy, but we also like to participate in all applications both online and offline. It's the way to make sense of everything and maintain consistency.

Our goal is to provide each brand, company or project with a solid, recognizable and unique identity. We approach each project as if it were our own, regardless of size or geographic location.

Still Young p.292 / p.346 / p.354 / p.362

https://www.behance.net/1b83e145

studio IeM p.028 / p.084 / p.140

This is Minseong Jeon from the visual director and brand experience design studio REM. Under the belief that good design cannot be achieved without deep insight, understanding, and sincere passion, we propose effective design solutions by in-depth analysis of the essence and results of each brand and the direction they pursue.

Studio Woork p.098 / p.146

Io Woo is a multi-disciplinary designer and creative director of Studio Woork, with a deep approach towards three causes of life: nature, design, and the people. If he can conclude his take on life, it would be 'one-great-design': waking up in the morning, getting things done in order, coexisting with time as a part of life. He exposes himself to social activities regularly, in the hope to connect, embracing, and finally giving back. He aims for a simple living, rooted side by side surrounded by nature and daily contemplations.

Tomas Mielnikowicz p.250

In 2006 he finished his secondary studies at the Philips school receiving the title of Bilingual Electromechanical Technician. Architect from the Architecture, Design and Urbanism University of Buenos Aires, Argentina (FADU - UBA) in 2013. He worked in several studios during his initial training period, including the MSGSSS studio (2010-2013). Teacher in the subject "Architecture II" in the Grinberg chair in the period 2014 - 2018, forming part of the teaching group together with members of the MONOBLOCK office. In 2015, he founded PALPA Arquitectura associated with 3 colleagues from the university, Sara Barugel, Lucia Boano and Julia Tavella, where they developed residential, commercial and hotel projects. In 2019, he separated from PALPA Arquitectura to continue developing independently in search of new challenges and new associations, expanding the spectrum of his work by interacting in a multidisciplinary way with other professions. He participated in various competitions independently (highlighting the second prize with the proposal for the science park and the third prize for the Argentine pavilion at the 2020 Venice Biennale), and associated with studios such as MSGSSS, DIEGUEZ&FRIDMAN, UNOENCINCO, etc.

Uido Design Studio

p.044 / p.074 / p.122 / p.184 / p.198

A selected group of multi-talented people creating all kinds of designs. We were friends when we started the studio, and we attracted great talents to be part of it, who become our friends now. We always prefer quality over quantity, period. If you start to work with us you can be sure we have the time to over deliver your expectations.

YRAD p.324

YRAD, based in Japan, was established in 2016 by Yuuki Tanaka (b. 1981, Japan) and Ryosuke Enomoto (b. 1981, Japan).

Yuuki Tanaka

Born in 1981. Graduated from Showa Woman's University, Faculty of Life and Environmental Sciences, Department of Human Environmental Sciences in 2003, and completed the master's program at the Graduate School of Showa Woman's University in 2005. After working at an architects office, established YRAD in 2016.

Ryosuke Enomoto

Born in 1981. Graduated from Kogakuin University, Faculty of Engineering Division II, Department of Architecture in 2005. After working at an architects office, established YRAD in 2016.

Image_ KAUFF ROASTERS_ Plainoddity

Enjoy Coffee2

Coffee Branding & Café Design

0123456789abcdefghijklmnopqrstuvwxyz